RADICAL
GENEROSITY

M. J. RYAN

RADICAL GENEROSITY

Unlock the Transformative Power of Giving

M. J. RYAN

FOREWORD BY SYLVIA BOORSTEIN, AUTHOR OF *IT'S EASIER THAN YOU THINK*
INTRODUCTION BY VICKI SAUNDERS, FOUNDER OF SHEEO

Conari Press

This edition first published in 2018 by Conari Press, an imprint of

Red Wheel/Weiser, LLC
With offices at:
65 Parker Street, Suite 7
Newburyport, MA 01950
www.redwheelweiser.com

Cover design by Kathryn Sky-Peck
Cover illustration by iStock.com
Interior by Deborah Dutton
Typeset in Janson Text LT Std, Trade Gothic LT Std, and FB Californian

Printed in Canada
MAR
10 9 8 7 6 5 4 3 2 1

*In honor of all my teachers of the heart,
particularly my father*

We make a living by what we get, but we make a life by what we give.

—NORMAN MACESWAN

Contents

CHAPTER 3
The Attitudes of Radical Generosity 41

CHAPTER 4
The Practices of Radical Generosity 89

CHAPTER 5
An Ever-Expanding Spiral 157

Foreword

In 1990, James Baraz and I traveled to India with some of our friends to visit the venerable Advaita teacher Sri H. W. L. Poonja in Lucknow. Every day for three weeks we traveled (on three-wheeled taxis, then pedal-rickshaw, then on foot) to arrive in time for morning darshan (teachings) with Poonjaji. We sat squeezed in close to each other on the floor of Poonjaji's small living room, along with perhaps twenty other students from all over the world. Poonjaji sat on a raised plat-form in the front of the room and talked and taught and laughed for hours, including each of us, one by one, in dialogue. We loved it. And at the end, Poonjaji agreed to see James and me in a private interview.

"What do you teach?" he asked.

James answered, "We teach Mindfulness and Metta, and we specifically emphasize *dana* (generosity)."

"There is no such thing as generosity," Poonjaji said. (James and I exchanged glances that said, "Uh-oh! Have we just started to present ourselves and done it wrong?")

"No such thing at all," Poonjaji continued. "There is only the arising of need and the natural impulse of the heart to address it. If you are hungry, and your hand puts food in your mouth, you don't think of the hand as generous, do you? If someone in front of you is hungry, and you put food in their mouth, it's the same, isn't it?"

James and I talked afterward. "Maybe he's right," I said. "Let's think this through. When I put away my winter clothing, I think, 'This I didn't wear at all: Salvation Army. This I wore a little bit. Hmmm. I could save it; I could give it to the Salvation Army. I'll give it away!' Isn't that generosity?"

"Maybe it's mindful-awareness-of-the-presence-of-lust or mindful-awareness-of-the-absence-of-lust," James said. "No *one* who is generous."

"Hmmm," I thought. I've continued to think about it for ten years.

I think there is no *one* who is generous, but there *is* generosity. Generosity is a habit of mind, a tendency, a capacity. It is the antidote for lust. It enables the

Radical Generosity

mind to relax when it gets tied in knots of clinging. It conditions thoughts like, "Maybe I *don't* need this," and "Probably I'll feel happier sharing." It does create happiness. When we feel we have enough, when we feel satisfied, when we feel, "My cup is brimming," we are unafraid. We are at ease. We are happy!

The Buddha named Generosity as the first of the Ten *Paramitas* (Perfected Qualities) of an enlightened mind. He suggested that people begin their conscious cultivation of the Paramitas with the practice of Generosity because it is the simplest. Everyone, he said, has something they could give away, and the act of giving brings gladness and joy to the mind. I was encouraged when I heard about *cultivating* Paramitas. It meant to me that I didn't need to wait until after enlightenment—if, and whenever, that might happen—to manifest these lovely qualities. And I was thrilled to hear accounts of many, many people, in the time of the Buddha, who became completely enlightened just by hearing him speak. The written accounts usually end with the phrase "and their minds, through not clinging, were liberated from taints." They had generous minds. They let go of their old views. They gave themselves the gift of freedom.

I also understand the nine other Paramitas, those that follow Generosity in the traditional list, as elaborated forms of Generosity. They are *all* gifts. Morality gives the people we meet the gift of safety and gives us what the Buddha called "the bliss of blamelessness." Renunciation gives us the gift of a calmed-down lust system, which moves us to cherish and appreciate what we already have. When we practice Restraint, we give ourselves the gift of self-confidence, the assurance that our impulse system will not take off on its own. When we are Patient, we give ourselves the gift of reflection and wise choice. When we are Honest, we give ourselves and the people with whom we are honest the gift of intimacy. When I give myself the gift of Energy—by taking quiet time in my days, retreat time in my life, bicycle time for my body—I reconnect with what I *know* to be true. The energy of that reconnection sustains my relationships with the people I meet.

If I am able to love and forgive myself—not always easy—I will be able to be a gift of kindness to anyone I meet. When I practice Equanimity—making my mind still enough and wide enough and balanced enough to hold the whole universe of stories with the Wisdom that sees them as conditioned links in a lawful cosmos

of connections—I am able to cry hard and laugh loud and feel whole.

Poonjaji was right about no *one* being generous. When I feel whole, when I don't feel needy, I forget myself. I share more. I become kinder. In the end, Generosity becomes the great Act of Kindness that sustains the world.

My grandfather lived with my family for some years when he was in his middle nineties. The story he liked most to tell, when people asked him how he liked living with us, was one in which Smokey, our very friendly old Labrador retriever, had once again gotten through the gate and made his way to the grade school three blocks away. The children there loved him, and the teachers used him as a therapy for children who had dog fears, but the Humane Society came by every morning and picked up all dogs off leashes, and Smokey had been "arrested" many times.

"The school called me," my grandfather would say, "and told me, 'Smokey is here. Come quickly before the Pound comes.' So I rushed to school as fast as I could with the leash, and the bell for the end of school rang just as Smokey and I were leaving. So, Emily walked with us."

Emily, my youngest child, was eight at the time. My grandfather was ninety-four.

He continued, "We had just started walking when suddenly it started to rain. Emily took off her raincoat"—at that point in the story my grandfather always started to cry—"and said, 'Here, Grandpa. You wear this.'"

That was the story he told most. Generosity stories, kindness stories, are the ones we all *must* tell most to keep our hearts and spirits alive in this most complicated and difficult and amazing life. The wonderful stories in this inspiring book both touched my heart and lifted my spirit. I am sure they will do the same for you.

—Sylvia Boorstein, author of *It's Easier Than You Think: The Buddhist Way to Happiness*

Why Radical Generosity?

I met MJ almost twenty years ago, and every single interaction with her over the years has been a deep learning experience. She creates the space for everyone she works with to find their path to their own wisdom, as she did with me around giving and receiving.

I remember the first time the concept of "radical generosity" came into my mind. I was thinking about what kind of environment would really support women in achieving their dreams through entrepreneurship. I'm a student of innovation ecosystems and of culture and behavior change. I had witnessed a number of different ecosystems when I was entrepreneuring—the exuberant, dreaming atmosphere in Prague, right after the wall fell down; the conservative, restricted vibe in Canada in the early '90s; and then the "anything is possible" Silicon Valley in the early 2000s. I'm obsessed with what it takes to create an environment for people to achieve beyond what they think is possible for themselves. What are the necessary conditions?

I'm also deeply aware of how challenging it is to be a woman in all of these systems. Women were not at the table to design our world, so surprise, surprise, it's not working so well for us. We are surrounded by incessant judgment, especially as women, that results in most of us living smaller and unplugging from the male-dominant culture we live in. The vast majority of women entrepreneurs keep their businesses under $1M in revenue because it's easier to stay small. We do it all ourselves rather than reach out in an unforgiving environment and be told we are not enough, we are not doing it right, we aren't bold enough or taking enough risk, and on and on.

It's super easy to be grumpy right back at someone who is grumpy to you, to be intolerant of someone who isn't as fast as you or as smart as you, and on and on. It's easy to say, "it's just business, nothing personal" as an excuse to treat people badly.

But what if we were starting over? How would we design this world from a more balanced perspective? A perspective that works for more than simply the

"winners"? What if we could create an entrepreneurial environment, and ultimately a society, that works for all? What would our cultural environment be? I played with this question for years and have had thousands of conversations exploring another path forward.

What if people supported us on our own terms?

What if we started from the premise that we are all doing our best at any given time?

What if we lifted people up instead of pushing them down, pouncing on the first mistake made?

What if we trusted instead of trying to control everything?

What if we didn't discard everything that isn't "hard" and "measurable" by calling it "soft" or "intangible"?

What if women don't need to be fixed but actually offer the solution, the balance, to our totally out of whack winner-takes-all world? What if we created a different environment, one that was designed specifically to support and elevate women's strengths?

Everything about this world is made up. We could just as easily change it.

Women are collaborative, supportive, giving and focused on improving humanity. I want to live in a

Why Radical Generosity?

world that celebrates these attributes. The word that kept coming up over and over again when I thought about how to help change the world was "generosity." Knowing what I know about the world, I thought it needed to have more of an edge to resonate with our current reality. Something stronger. So I began talking about the concept of "Radical Generosity."

What if we were radically generous to women who have world-changing ideas? Would we walk into that relationship expecting a return? I think not. Those questions led me to launch, with the help of many radically generous women, SheEO, an organization in which women activate their capital, their networks, their expertise, and their buying power—without expectation of a return—on behalf of women entrepreneurs who have ventures that are creating a better world. And I engaged MJ to be one of the leaders of the guided development program for the chosen entrepreneurs that is one of the key elements of the model.

The results? All of us are emboldened, dreaming bigger, growing ourselves, our ventures, our leadership. We are dreaming together, cocreating a space where we can all achieve our dreams, lifting each other up, finding deeper meaning, asking ourselves:

Radical Generosity

Can I be doing more? Can I have a bigger positive impact? What am I here to give?

When I first began this journey, Radical Generosity felt like a stretch, a curiosity, a moonshot, almost. But the more I talk about it and practice it, the more it transforms my life. It began with me asking, moment to moment, "What is the radically generous response now?" What is the radically generous response to that "crusty" email? To that person who is asking a big favor? What if I was radically generous with myself today? How would I act differently? How would I solve this issue if I thought I was surrounded by radically generous women who are connected to everything I need?

When I first spoke to my mom about the concept of radical generosity, she said, "Really, Vicki, why 'radical'? It's simply generosity." But my mom was always radically generous. She was wildly off the charts in this area. That for me was and is the bar. My mom. Radical Generosity.

Over the past two and a half years, I have built up my ability to frame most of my actions around radical generosity. The result? I'm happier. I'm healthier. I'm nicer. I'm less stressed. I let go of things I can't control

Why Radical Generosity?

much more quickly. I'm literally a new person. I feel like I have a whole lot more, of everything, than I ever did before. An abundance of resources, of energy, of love, of wisdom. By being nicer to myself and others, I'm happier. Seriously, I know this is not rocket science, this simple action you can take, and yet it literally changes your life when you do it.

One of the things I have learned since practicing radical generosity is that it requires you to both give and receive to be complete. As MJ says, "Giving and receiving are like the in breath and the out breath. You need both to be whole."

I never liked to receive. I am a big giver, like many women I know. I've learned from MJ and from experience that if you give without receiving, you always feel "lack." And you begin to resent that fact that no one else seems to give to you. The challenge of receiving is that you have to be open to it, and you have to ask for help, something we know many women do not like to do.

There is a funny Amy Schumer skit in which she compliments someone on what they are wearing and they say, "Oh, this? I got it for $10 at Target." Rather than say thank you and receive the compliment, we

literally push it away and diminish it. And if you follow that through, speaking for myself here, I diminish myself every time I don't accept from others.

Every woman I know wants to give to others and help others; by not accepting that generosity and support, I rob her of that happiness. By not accepting your compliment, support, love, or offer of help, I isolate myself and remove the chance of a deeper connection with you. And all we really want is deeper connections and stronger relationships with one another. We are desperately missing humanity in this world, a deeper sense of connection with each other, a yearning for community, for trust; radical generosity is the path I chose to take to get there.

MJ has written a comprehensive guide on the gifts you get, the attitudes you hold, and the practices you can perform when you choose to become radically generous. I hope this book helps you to find your way toward your potential, to deeper relationships, and to a happier life as it did for me.

Enjoy.

—Vicki Saunders, founder of SheEO

Why Radical Generosity?

CHAPTER 1

Opening Our Hearts and Hands

Above all let us never forget that an act of goodness is an act of happiness.

—COUNT MAURICE MAETERLINCK

I was sitting in a café one day, waiting for a friend, when I noticed a middle-aged woman walking toward a nearby table, juggling three cups of coffee and the paraphernalia that goes along with them. She handed two of the cups over to two gentlemen who were sitting there. "Thank you," one of them said. "My pleasure," she replied and flashed such a radiant smile that I knew down to my bones that her simple act had brought her pleasure, and even happiness.

If you are like me, you want to be happy. Like me, you've probably spent a lot of time trying to be happy. Are you? As study after study has found over the past decades, the number of Americans who consider themselves happy has been steadily declining. There are many reasons for this—the world is increasingly more complex and challenging; we have all sorts of economic, environmental, political and social challenges. These are real and should not be underestimated.

The good news is that these challenges give us an opportunity to re-imagine the world and ourselves. That's why I am so excited to be involved with SheEO, as Vicki Saunders describes in the introduction. But we can't change the outside world if we don't transform ourselves internally as well. And I know that's possible, because I did it myself.

I don't profess to have all the answers. All I know is that in my twenties and thirties, I was your average unhappy and fearful person. Then, about twenty-five years ago, through a series of circumstances, I began to refocus my life on what truly mattered and stopped being miserable. And that's made all the difference.

It started when I, along with several others, published the book *Random Acts of Kindness*.™ It seemed like a good idea at the time—let's all do nice little things for strangers—but once I began to see and hear about its effects, I sensed I had stumbled upon

something very important. Suddenly I was inundated by letters from people telling me about the joy they had experienced as either doers or receivers of these acts. I will never forget the letter from a high school student who said he was going to kill himself until he read our book and decided that life was worth living. I became fascinated by the power of kindness and went on to help write a series of books on the topic. I tried to enact what I was writing about and became more kind both to strangers and to those I am close to. Like the boy who didn't kill himself, I got happier.

I began to wonder about the other qualities that could produce the same positive effect as kindness and turned my attention to gratitude. The more I cultivated a sense of appreciation for all that I had instead of focusing on what I lacked, the happier and less fearful I was. I wrote about my experiences, this time in *Attitudes of Gratitude*, and, once again, I received many letters about the power gratitude has in bringing peace of mind and a sense of contentment.

As soon as I finished *Attitudes of Gratitude*, my mind immediately moved to generosity, the spontaneous giving of ourselves and our resources to someone else. In a sense, I have now come full circle. Generosity is the

Opening Our Hearts and Hands

mother of kindness. Our desire to give help, comfort, support, or appreciation is often the reason we do kind things. And gratitude and generosity are two halves of an experience we don't have a word for, at least not one I've ever found. With gratitude, we take in the fullness of our lives and naturally want to give back from that overflow.

Vicki has helped me see that the act of generosity is indeed a radical one. Maurice Maeterlinck alludes to the power of generosity in the quote at the beginning of this chapter. We tend to think about generosity as volunteering or giving money or time, but generosity is actually much broader. It comes in all kinds of forms—material, intellectual, emotional, and spiritual. We can be generous when we give our knowledge, our awareness, our empathy, or our silence. Generosity is also about letting go of grudges, hurts, and concepts of ourselves and the world that stand in the way of our connection to others.

Radical generosity is openheartedness, the experience and expression of our boundless, unconditionally loving nature. It is such an important concept that Buddhists consider its opposite to be delusion. When we are out of touch with our giving hearts, the

natural flow of generosity within us, we think we need to hold on to money, possessions, and fixed ideas. We are sure we need these things to be happy, when our very grasping and clinging is what makes us miserable. We hold on so tightly that our hands are unavailable to reach out for the happiness we could gain by letting go. Our delusion of material happiness prevents us from being truly happy.

However, when we are living from true generosity, we feel expansive and abundant. We know that we can find true happiness in loving and being loved to the core of our being. Our hearts and hands are open, ready to offer what they can and able to receive what comes back to us in return.

As the woman in the café realized, giving makes us feel great. It's a fabulous feeling, even when we offer something as small as a cup of coffee. Giving lifts us out of our preoccupation with ourselves and reminds us that there is plenty of kindness to go around.

Like kindness and gratitude, giving—both of ourselves and our unique gifts—is actually very simple. So simple that it's often difficult to believe it can bring us such joy. We think giving should be hard, so we make it complicated. We guilt-trip ourselves into thinking

Opening Our Hearts and Hands

we should give more or try harder, usually turning our guilt into shame, and then trying to avoid the whole issue entirely.

It doesn't have to be that way. The purpose of this book is to provide encouragement. Encouragement in noticing that the river of generosity is already flowing in you, and encouragement in opening your heart as much as you feel comfortable and giving exactly as much as you want. It's about paying attention and noticing how you feel when you give, when it feels good and when it doesn't. Noticing the effects on your life and then choosing to do more of what makes you feel good.

I've come to understand that generosity is both a feeling—of fullness, of expansion, of joy—and a choice. The more we make the choice, the more we experience the feeling. This book charts a journey through attitudes and behaviors that I hope will allow you to open your heart more easily and frequently.

I am not setting myself up as an expert. If you met me, I don't think you'd be particularly struck by my generosity. Regard me as a fellow seeker on the path, a person who has often been quite fearful and stingy but who wants to change. Recently I read a novel

about a girl with "a heart so clear you could see all the way through it." That's how openhearted I want to be. I've seen, and even tasted a bit for myself, the peace, joy, and sense of contentment that the giving heart can offer, and I want us all to share in more of that contentment.

I'm convinced that we are here on Earth to grow our souls, to open wider, to reach higher, and to stretch farther. Our goal is to soften where we would normally constrict, to loosen when we would habitually tighten, and to extend where we would usually hold back. Each and every one of us has so much to offer, and the world needs what we have to give.

Opening Our Hearts and Hands

CHAPTER 2

The Gifts of Radical Generosity

Radical generosity has raised my awareness around where I have tended to play small due to my self-limiting beliefs, where I make choses out of fear/scarcity versus love and abundance towards myself.

—GOLNAZ GOLNARAGHI, SHEEO ACTIVATOR

We begin by examining the bounty generosity can bring. Understanding the rewards we will reap may motivate us to cultivate our own gifts and offer them wholeheartedly to the world. As we discover the grace that comes of giving, we begin to experience generosity as a natural upwelling of the heart that exists in each of us, and as a limitless treasure that can bring us immeasurable delight.

Giving Is a Great Mood Elevator

No joy can equal the joy of serving others.

—SAI BABA

It was one of those no-good rotten days in which nothing was going right for me. I had been up half the night with my daughter Ana, my computer kept crashing, and I got ten phone calls that distracted me from my writing. When I picked Ana up from preschool, I was in a less than stellar mood. I popped her into the car, and, still grumbling to myself, we headed for the grocery store.

At the store, the line seemed interminable. Finally I was the next one up, but it was still taking forever. Despite my annoyance, I tuned in to what was happening. The young woman in front of me kept asking the cashier to give her the total after each item. She had a tiny baby in her cart, and it was clear she didn't have enough money to pay for all the food she bought, so she went off to make a phone call, presumably to ask someone for money.

While she was gone, I asked the cashier to total up everything and tell her that she had enough money.

I would make up the difference when she left. The cashier asked me if I knew her—1 didn't—and then if I were wealthy. "Yes," I replied, thinking of my beautiful daughter, the roof over my head, and the privilege of doing work that I loved.

When I left the store, I realized I was singing along with the radio and feeling remarkably good. The best part of the situation was that the woman never realized what I had done. A bit puzzled, she had gladly wheeled her cart away. I smiled to myself. Reaching out to her had reset my mood, and I felt like I was in love with the whole world.

Recent research backs up my experience. In a study done at the University of Zurich, volunteers who agreed to give away twenty-five Swiss francs reported feeling significantly happier than those who spent the same amount on themselves.

Helping others really is a "feel good" pill. When I was doing the research for my book, *365 Health and Happiness Boosters*, I realized that making someone else happy creates happiness the fastest. Lending a hand, making someone smile, or being of use to someone other than ourselves helps us stop focusing solely on our own difficulties and gives a larger perspective to

our days. This is what Karl Marx meant when he said, "Experience praises the most happy the one who made the most people happy."

Giving Can Heal

There is a wonderful, mystical law of nature that the three things we crave most in life—happiness, freedom, and peace of mind—are always attained by giving them to someone else.

—ANONYMOUS

During the breakup of a fourteen-year relationship, I was in terrible pain and leaned heavily on the love and advice of my friends, including author Daphne Rose Kingma, who flew up from Santa Barbara to sit with me for a few days. When she was about to leave, she gave me a tiny piece of paper, her prescription for my healing: (1) Go to therapy; (2) Meditate; (3) Reach out to others in pain.

I'm glad to say I did all three items. At the time, though, I didn't see why helping others would help me. I understood the benefits of therapy—working through the grief, coming to see my part in the

break-up, and understanding the relationship dynamics I tend to encounter. I saw how meditation might work—tapping into the sense of peacefulness and wholeness beneath the pain of my situation. But giving to others? Wasn't this a time to focus on myself?

Once I began to volunteer at a "Meals on Wheels" organization for people with AIDS, I learned that giving to others was also a way to help myself. Helping others forced me to notice something other than my own misery, which was a great gift. Rather than wallowing in all the ways I had been mistreated and abused, I could turn my attention to someone else. As months passed, however, I discovered something else. Walking the halls of the welfare hotel where most of my deliveries were, I stopped being so attached to my particular wound and began to see that suffering is part of life. All kinds of terrible things happen to people, often for no reason, and I was not specially singled out for victimization.

While it wasn't true for me in this situation, giving when you are feeling hurt often makes meaning out of your suffering. The person who's paralyzed by a gunshot wound and then becomes an advocate for gun control, the woman who finally escapes from her

The Gifts of Radical Generosity

abusive husband and works to set up a shelter for battered women—these are individuals who reach up out of the particulars of their individual tragedies to ensure that others will not have to suffer the same fate.

You don't have to be suffering from some specific hurt to reap the benefits of giving. Any time we reach out to others—in our hurt or with our love—we feel better.

Giving Is Good for Our Health

It is one of the most beautiful compensations of life that no (hu)man can sincerely try to help another without helping himself.

—RALPH WALDO EMERSON

I have a friend who has had a terrible case of lupus for nearly twenty years. She has been hospitalized many times and is constantly on medication that has horrible side effects, including cataracts. She had to quit her job as a graphic designer and now is completely supported by her husband. She can get really down about her life. Recently she decided to become a volunteer at a soup kitchen. She goes when she feels up to it, and she's

started to discover that the more she goes, the better she feels—emotionally and physically. Her arthritis (a consequence of lupus) isn't as severe and she has more energy.

Helping others not only can make us feel good about ourselves; it can also increase our physical well-being. The mind and body aren't separate. Anything we do to elevate our spirits will also have a beneficial effect on our health. A study by Cornell University found that volunteering increases a person's energy, sense of mastery over life, and self-esteem. Other studies have demonstrated that such positive feelings can actually strengthen and enhance the immune system. Positive emotions increase the body's number of T-cells, cells in the immune system that help the body resist disease and recover quickly from illness. Positive emotions also release endorphins into the bloodstream. Endorphins are the body's natural tranquilizers and painkillers; they stimulate dilation of the blood vessels, which leads to a relaxed heart.

While we don't quite understand all the reasons why giving creates good health, many studies have documented generosity's positive effects. Michigan researchers who studied twenty-seven hundred people

The Gifts of Radical Generosity

15

for almost ten years found that men who regularly did volunteer work had death rates two and a half times lower than men who didn't. In a separate study, volunteers who worked directly with those who benefited from their services had a greater immune system boost than those whose volunteer work was restricted to pushing papers.

Harvard researchers also conducted a study that showed how giving is such a powerful immune booster that it can be experienced just by watching someone else in the act of giving! In this well-known experiment, students looking at a film of Mother Teresa as she tended the sick in Calcutta—even those who purported to dislike Mother Teresa—got an increase in immune function.

Psychologist Robert Ornstein and physician David Sobel are well known for their examinations of the health effects of altruism. In their book *Healthy Pleasures*, they describe what they call the "helper's high," a kind of euphoria volunteers get when helping others—a warm glow in the chest and a sense of vitality that comes from being simultaneously energized and calm. They compare it to a runner's high and claim it is caused by the body's release of endorphins.

Because of all these health benefits, as Stella Reznick says in *The Pleasure Zone*, "the one who ends up getting the most from a good deed may, ultimately, be the good Samaritan."

Generosity Alleviates Fear

It is expressly at those times when we feel needy that we will benefit the most from giving.

—RUTH ROSS

I've never had the privilege of meeting writer Anne Lamott, but I have loved her books, particularly *Operating Instructions*. Her emotional honesty leaps off every page—here is a woman who is not afraid to show herself, warts and all. In admitting her vulnerabilities, she makes it okay for us to be just who we are, too.

In an interview, she was asked about her relationship to money. As a single mother living off her writing, her financial security has been precarious at best. She spoke of having survived, at times, off the generosity of friends, and then said something that leaped out at me. "I know that if I feel any deprivation or fear [about money], the solution is to give. The solution is

to go find some mothers on the streets of San Raphael and give them tens and twenties and mail off another $50 to Doctors Without Borders to use for the refugees in Kosovo. Because I know that giving is the way we can feel abundant. Giving is the way that we fill ourselves up. . . . For me the way to fill up is through service and sharing and getting myself to give more than I feel comfortable giving."

To me, a person who has a great deal of fear when it comes to money, the thought of giving money away precisely when I felt like clinging to it seemed terrifying. Sick of constantly being fearful about money, I decided to give it a try. Amazingly, it really works. I feel less afraid the more I give.

It's a paradox. If we are afraid of not having enough, we think we need to hold on tightly to what we have and work hard to get more. As Anne Lamott and I found out, that perspective only makes us more afraid, because we get caught in a cycle of clinging and hoarding. When is enough enough? Is $5,000 enough? $50,000? $100,000? $1 million? A recent study found that no matter how much money people made, they thought they would be happier if only they had more.

Radical Generosity

Whether they made $20,000 a year or $200,000, everyone thought they needed a bit more.

If we turn around and give instead of hoarding everything, we suddenly experience the abundance we do have. Most of us, particularly those of us living in Western societies, have a great deal, and when we share what we have, we feel our abundance. It becomes real to us, and that diminishes our fears. I read about a woman who was suffering from depression and contemplating suicide because of back pain and poverty. She found a kid foraging in a dumpster and thought to herself, "I don't have a lot, but at least I can fix this kid a peanut butter sandwich." Giving away that peanut butter sandwich reminded her of the abundance she still had, even in the projects. If she could still give, her life wasn't so bleak after all. She now runs a volunteer program in Dallas that feeds hundreds of kids a day. It started from that one day when she gave away the sandwich.

The Gifts of Radical Generosity

Giving Helps Us Experience Our Connection with Others

Just as the wave cannot exist for itself, but is ever a part of the heaving surface of the ocean, so must I never live my life for itself, but always in the experience which is going on all around me.

—ALBERT SCHWEITZER

My friend Tom recently went to his high school reunion and had a surprising experience. "I always thought reunions were stupid," he said, "and so I never went. But an old friend called and guilt-tripped me into it, so I went. It was strange, but not in the way I had imagined.

"I'm a very successful financial analyst, a bit on the driven side, but it got me all the things I thought I wanted—a great condo in the city, a country house, fancy car. So I showed up with a bit of a self-satisfied attitude. There were plenty of surprises, both in appearance—people change a lot in twenty years— and in what individuals had done with their lives. The biggest surprise was that the people who seemed the most happy were not those who had 'made it' in

the sense that I would have understood. There were a number of people in my income bracket—lawyers, computer guys—but for the most part they were the most unhappy and lonely.

"The interaction that really affected me was with an old girlfriend who was a nursery school teacher. When she talked about 'her kids,' her eyes would light up with a kind of excitement and energy I hadn't seen for years.

"It came to me that she had a very deep connection to the people in her work life—kids, parents, and other teachers—that came out of her giving them her time, energy, and enthusiasm; whereas I had all the trimmings of a great life but wasn't connected to anything at all except my wallet. That was the beginning of my midlife crisis, and it hasn't been easy. I decided to take a small step and become a Big Brother to a twelve-year-old kid from the projects. I've been really enjoying myself, taking him to ball games and helping with homework."

The wonderful thing about giving is that you can't help but experience a good feeling when you do it. Humans are social creatures. We're made to live within the company of others, and initiating that

connection—making it concrete—just feels good in and of itself. When we get narrowly focused on just ourselves, we lose track of the sense of connection to others that helping gives us and instead experience isolation and loneliness. Far too many of us are stuck in that state today. Cut off from enough meaningful contact, we drift alone in the universe. No matter our circumstances, we can always experience human connection simply by reaching out to help someone else. When it comes to connecting, what you give is what you'll get.

Giving Allows Us to Look Deeply at Ourselves

Just as we are, we are giving and receiving life. But we miss this because we are caught up with all of the efforts to be right, to be the best, to be the winner, to be first. All the evaluations and judgments we make about ourselves and others separate us from this simple being.

—ROBERT JOSHIN ALTHOUSE SENSEI

For three years, I delivered dinner once a week to people with AIDS. I would go to the distribution point,

pick up ten or fifteen packaged meals, get a piece of paper that showed me the addresses of where to go, and set off. For three years, I watched my reactions to the very simple act of delivering food, and I learned a lot about myself.

People with chronic illnesses tend to be worse off financially, and it was certainly true of the folks on my route. I was required to drive in the "worst" part of town, and it was usually dark when I made my rounds. My first reaction was fear. After a few weeks, I became somewhat comfortable, and the fear mostly receded into the background. Sometimes if I were walking down the long, dark corridor of a welfare hotel, I would fear the thought of someone grabbing me, raping me, and infecting me with AIDS.

Most of the time, what I felt was pride. Wasn't I a "good" person to be doing such a thing? Wasn't I brave, generous, even saintly? Every time I delivered the meals, I had a story line about my virtuous behavior running in my head. I was so caught up with myself that on more than one occasion, I missed a chance to be truly helpful because I was so caught up in either my fear or my grandiose thoughts.

The Gifts of Radical Generosity

My goal with this story is to point out that giving triggers all kinds of thoughts and feelings. Examining them can be useful to our personal development—we learn more if we adopt an "Oh, isn't that interesting" approach to what we discover instead of bludgeoning ourselves with "Aren't I terrible." My experience with the meals showed me how much I want to *look* good—especially to myself.

What should you do with what you discover about yourself? Acknowledge it—you really need to think of yourself as a good person. Have compassion for it. Don't try to fix or change it. Just hold the truth in the spaciousness of your being. By accepting it instead of denying it, pushing it away, trying to make it be different, or forcing yourself into some other position, you create the space for it to transform. Even if it never changes, at least you are aware of it, and you're being generous regardless of your motivation. In the end, the good we do is much more significant than any mixed motives we might have.

Generosity Helps Us See
There Is No Difference Between
Giving and Receiving

Each day as we embrace the sun with love and joy, we can come to the realization that giving and receiving are the same. Therefore, we will give equally without reservation.

—AEESHA ABABIO-CLOTTEY AND
KOKOMON CLOTTEY

In the book *Beyond Fear*, social worker Aeesha Ababio-Clottey tells this story. Every day, on her way to and from work, she passed the same homeless person begging at the entrance to the subway. Rushing past, she would never even look at him, much less put a penny in his cup. One evening, she was a dime short for the ticket that would get her home. "I looked around," she wrote, "and everyone was in a hurry, trying to get home. . . . And as I looked, people avoided eye contact, with the unspoken message: Don't ask me."

Finally, in her desperation, she turned to the beggar and asked to borrow a dime. He insisted she take a quarter. Then she inquired if he had a place to live and told him about the treatment center where she worked

and how she could help him. "I'm quite happy, thank you," he replied. "I meet all kinds of people here, and I really enjoy myself, and I don't want to change it."

What a morality play! The professional "giver," the social worker, has ignored the professional "receiver," the beggar, for months. Then she ends up having to receive from him, and discovers that while he has no use for what she has to give, he has what she needs.

It's easy in the giving position to assume a sense of superiority—I, in my benevolence, will assist you, you poor thing. This creates all kinds of problems: The receiver can fall into a sense of inferiority and dependence that often creates anger and resentment, while the giver develops an inflated ego and a false sense of independence. When we remember that at any given moment we might be in need of help, though, we can then offer our services on a more equal level.

As we open our hearts, we come to see that there is really no difference between giving and receiving. They are just two sides of the experience, because neither can exist without the other. It is like imagining breathing without both the inhaling (receiving) and the exhaling (giving). Perhaps if we had a word for the experience of giving that encompasses both aspects,

we would see it for what it truly is—one act with two parts, both honorable, both crucial.

Giving Fills Us Like Getting Cannot

For many years, I was a man riding an ox, looking for an ox to ride on.

—MEISTER ECKHART

I once was talking about the nature of addiction with an acquaintance who is, by her definition, a food addict. She said that she overate because she felt there was a hole in the center of her being. "The difference between me and you, Mary Jane," she said, "is that you know the hole can't be filled, and I keep thinking it can be filled with food."

For me, this was one of those remarks that comes with lights around it: Pay attention, this is important. I've thought a lot about that hole over the years, and I am convinced that most of us have this sense of emptiness. We spend our lives trying to fill the hole with money, prestige, power, or even material objects. We think that if we get enough stuff, the hole will be filled, and our desire will be satiated.

The Gifts of Radical Generosity

This approach is not surprising, considering we live in a culture that survives on our consumerism. The economy booms when sales surge because we're throwing our money around; the economy falters when sales drop because we rein ourselves in. Every single day, on the radio, TV, the Internet, billboards, and in magazines and newspapers, we are encouraged and enticed to buy, buy, buy. Brilliant people create very sophisticated ads to convince us that if only we had this car, this computer, this Internet server, this toothpaste, or this brand of soap, we would be happy and fulfilled. It's only natural that we are focused on getting the red Porsche, the four thousand square-foot house, or the Ben & Jerry's ice cream.

Our desire will never disappear, because stuff can't fill the hole, no matter how much we get. Books and magazines are always filled with stories of folks who "had it all" yet were miserable. Our desires may change—we get the beautiful girl, the horse, or the million dollars in the bank, so now we want more friends, a child, or a vacation home—but they don't go away because desire is a natural part of the human condition. The problem isn't with our desire but, like

the reasoning of my friend the overeater, in thinking that the things we desire will fill the hole.

The answer is found in giving, not getting. If we tap into the natural sense of abundance that exists in each of us instead of focusing on filling the hole, we will be filled. It's a paradox—by focusing on getting, we remain forever empty; by focusing on giving, we become full. This idea is hard to accept because it goes against our cultural upbringing. I know that part of me is still convinced that the hole is not filled because I just haven't gotten the right things. If I did, this part says, then I would be happy.

As I have both gotten more and given more, I've realized that generosity is the true creator of happiness and peace of mind. As the Buddhist teacher Jack Kornfield once said, "Do you know any really generous people who aren't happy?" The real way to discover this truth, however, is to try it yourself. Try opening your heart and giving, particularly when you feel the hole in the center of your being. Magically it disappears, at least for a little while, as the love from your heart pours into it and into the world.

The Gifts of Radical Generosity

Giving Allows Us to Offer
Our Unique Gifts

*Every person born in this world represents something
new, something that never existed before, something
original and unique.*

—MARTIN BUBER

The ancient Greeks and Romans believed each human was born with a tutelary, or guardian, spirit inside us, a being that embodied our true essence. It was our task in life to set this spirit free so that our unique gifts could become manifest. The Greeks called this being a person's *daemon*, the Romans called it the *genius* (from the same Latin root as generosity—*genere*, which means to beget or produce). Socrates, for example, was believed to have a daemon who would speak up if he was about to do something that went counter to his essence. In Rome, it was customary to offer a sacrifice to your genius on your birthday, not to only receive gifts for yourself on that day but to give something to your guiding spirit. According to their beliefs, this being comes to us when we are born, and it carries the fullness of our undeveloped potential. If you cultivate

your gifts, the genius will become a household god when you die. If you ignore your potential, it will turn into a larva upon your death, a ghost that preys on the living.

These ancient beliefs match my own—we each are born with unique gifts to offer the world (*genius* is a synonym for gift), and our task in life is to discover our gifts and actualize them. This task is like a hero's journey more than any kind of small feat. As Marianne Williamson once said, "It takes more courage sometimes to face our greatness than it does to face our weakness."

In our culture, we are not taught how to recognize our gifts, much less manifest them. We are taught to have goals—graduate from high school, go to college, get married, raise a family—but not how to discover our unique purpose. Who in our childhood encouraged us to answer the questions: What do you love? What are you here to give? Even as adults, many of us have trouble even recognizing our unique talents and abilities. Often when I ask people to name their gifts, they look at me blankly.

Like the Greeks and Romans, I believe that discovering these gifts is the task of our lifetime. Through

The Gifts of Radical Generosity

our generosity, we can begin to see the shadow of our unique genius and offer it to the world. The nature of a gift is that it demands to be given. If we keep it to ourselves and fail to offer it to others, it dies unfulfilled.

Think back to what the Romans believed. If we release our gifts, then we will have succeeded in our life's purpose and the genius (our self) will become a god. If however, we fail to release our gifts, we will become hungry ghosts, harassing the living forever. Perhaps our ghosts harass the living because we are finally trying to give but can't because we are dead. While we're alive, though, it is never too late to share these gifts. What makes you feel most alive when you are sharing it'? Figuring this out will lead you to your particular gifts and your purpose for being alive.

Generosity Connects Us to Nature

Consider, too, the generous gifts of the natural world: beauty, protection, abundance, and resources from trees, plants, flowers, and the animals that share our fragile planet.

—KAY CHORAO

Although I'm originally from New England, I've lived in California for over forty years. Every year, I am still surprised by spring arriving in February. You'd think I would have reset my internal clock by now, but each February, when the plum trees burst into fuchsia hues, the daffodils push out their sunny heads, and the quince bushes show their salmon flowers, I am amazed.

Today, I took a break from writing to walk around my neighborhood and revel in spring. With the topic of generosity on my mind, I couldn't help but notice how bountiful and generous nature is. The blossoms on the plum tree are profuse, in excess of what is needed to produce fruit. The fruit in the summer will be bountiful; a few years ago a plum tree I had was so laden with fruit that a branch broke off from the sheer weight. My family and everyone in my office feasted on plums for weeks and weeks.

The life-force is inherently generous—in the wealth of different life forms as well as the profusion of blossoms, fruit, and seed—and all these forms depend on one another. The rabbit eats the flowers, the mountain lion eats the rabbit, when the lion dies it becomes compost that fertilizes the tree that produces the flower, and on and on. Every player in the cycle

literally lives off the others, with only the sun outside the process—giving but not receiving.

We are a part of this cycle, and our generosity is simply part of the great wheel of life. Our whole life can be viewed as a continuous cycle of transaction. We receive bounty from others—love, wisdom, lessons, and support as well as food, clothing, and shelter. After pausing to appreciate what we've been given and perhaps polishing those gifts that are slightly tarnished, we pass them on to other recipients. This is the essence of the web of life. All of creation, from the tiniest particle to the greatest mountain, is involved in this generous and continual exchange of energy.

When we give, we take our place in the order of things, and we experience our deep connection to all of nature. Giving is natural; we don't have to hoard it. In this cycle, it's as though we are standing in a giant line, receiving with one hand and passing what we received on to the next. Thus, giving—of ourselves and our resources—is a profound reminder that we are not separate from the natural world but an integral and responsible part of it.

Giving Allows Us to Experience Oneness

Constantly remind yourself, "I am a member of the whole body of conscious things." If you think of yourself as a mere "part," then love for humanity will not well up in your heart, you will look for some reward in every act of kindness and miss the boon which the act itself is offering. Then all your work will be seen as mere duty and not as the very porthole connecting you with the Universe itself.

—MARCUS AURELIUS

I was speaking in a classroom of third-graders one day about kindness and generosity. I asked the kids why we should do nice things for one another. Hands popped up: "Because it's the right thing to do." "Because it makes the other person feel good." "Because then they'll be nice to you." Then a girl in the corner said, "Because when you share with people, it makes you bigger; and when you don't share, it makes you smaller."

This child articulated something that even many adults never get. Giving makes us bigger. What I think she meant by bigger is that the very act of giving makes real the truth about life that mystics, sages, and

even certain scientists are trying to get us to understand—we are completely interconnected. Not really separate, even though it seems as though we are.

On one level, we are indeed each private, individual selves, making our way through life as best we can. In that realm, we are small. Even on this level, we can see the effects of our good deeds—a person who would otherwise go hungry is fed; a lost child is returned to her family; a forest is preserved.

At some other level, the nonmaterial level, there is no separation between me and the hungry person, me and the lost girl, or me and the trees. We are all, as Marcus Aurelius puts it, aspects of the vast body of consciousness that is life itself. On this level, we are huge.

This truth is beyond the realm of our ordinary experience and is often difficult to talk about. Many people talk in generalities about oneness and lack of separation. I believe that such lack of separateness has to be experienced to be understood, which is why the practice of generosity is so important. The more we live out of our generosity, the more we experience this larger self. Being more aware of our oneness will eventually help us make wiser decisions about life.

Generosity Helps Us Glimpse the Truth About Life

We live in a universe where relationships are primary. . . . Nothing exists independent of its relationships. We are constantly creating the world—evoking it from many potentials—as we participate in all its many interactions.

—MARGARET J. WHEATLEY

For centuries, we lived with the model that the world is a machine, and if we don't expend a great deal of energy keeping it and ourselves going in an orderly fashion, it will run down like a clock that has not been wound. According to theorist Margaret J. Wheatley, this view is of a universe "that cannot be trusted with its own processes for growth and rejuvenation."

Beginning in the 20th century, however, scientists began to discover that this view of the world was wrong. These scientists have begun to understand that life is inherently orderly and that it is in a constant process of creating and renewing itself. Everything alive is a living system, inextricably growing and

changing inside a vast, self-renewing, living system of life itself.

This awareness of how life actually works has tremendous implications for all aspects of human endeavors—everything from how businesses should be organized to how we can relate to one another personally. Because this worldview is only a hundred years old, we have just begun to incorporate the truth of it into our lives.

Generosity has a tremendous role in this new worldview. The practice of generosity allows people to experience the ways life really works: Nothing exists alone but only in relationship, and the future is not preordained but is brought about through the creation of relationships. When we reach out to others, for instance, we actually create the future through our giving and our interaction.

Think about it this way: You are a schoolteacher longing to make a difference for students who are having a hard time learning to read through conventional methods. One day you go to a party, even though you don't really feel like going. At the party, you meet a man, a computer programmer, who is also yearning to have more of an impact on the world. You and he have

an intense conversation about your ideas for teaching reading. You two really connect on this idea and meet several other times; finally, you work together to create a revolutionary new literacy website that really takes off, helping thousands of kids learn to read. If you hadn't talked to that man at the party, the website would never have been born, and many kids would have stayed functionally illiterate. Your interaction with him, however, resulted in that website, and, in a small way, you helped determine a brighter future for certain students.

Generosity is all about relationships, about creating and enacting connections, and about trusting that what goes around comes around. The more you experience generosity, the more you will experience how the good you do comes back to you in some form or another.

CHAPTER 3

The Attitudes of Radical Generosity

*Learning to embrace radical generosity has been
a catalyst to help me cultivate faith and fearlessness in all
aspects of life—especially the really scary ones.*

—MELINDA GONZALEZ, SHEEO ACTIVATOR

This section explores the attitudes that cultivate the openheartedness that is found in a giving heart. For some of us, such attitudes are innate, or they were taught to us when we were so young that they seem second nature now. For others of us, these attitudes may require some rethinking of our fundamental assumptions about life. Attitudes support behavior—we behave in certain ways because we believe certain things. If we change our minds, we can change our lives. All it takes is a willingness to change. It's a matter of figuring out what brings us true contentment—

whether it's believing that there isn't enough to go around, and we must hold on tight to what we have and look for more; or whether it's trusting that as we open our hearts to ourselves and others, we will be constantly replenished with love and the sense of fulfillment that comes only from sharing our gifts.

We Are Inherently Generous

Let's share.

—ANA LI, AGE THREE

One morning, when my child was three, she wanted potato chips for breakfast (I wasn't too strict when it comes to food). She took four chips, then gave me one of her four. "Let's share," she said. During this phase, whenever she ate something, she always gave me part of it, whether I wanted it or not.

Flash to the afternoon. We'd been to the store and she was climbing back in her car seat. She hated being strapped in, so the car seat was public enemy number one. She balked and jumped up and down on the seat. When I said, "Ana, please sit down, because someone is waiting for this parking space," she turned, saw the

car, and instantly sat. That wasn't unusual either; she quickly took her seat whenever someone was waiting.

I've thought a lot about the meaning of these behaviors. Conventional child-rearing wisdom says that kids are inherently possessive and self-centered, and that they need to be taught to share and to be considerate to others. I've learned from my experience that children, just as adults, can have feelings of "Mine, you can't have it" and "I want you to also enjoy this thing that I have," or feelings of "I want it exactly my way" and "What's good for you?" Selfishness and consideration exist in all of us. They are natural tendencies, two sides of the human coin. (Even scientists admit that humans developed both self-serving behavior and a genuine desire to help others because groups whose members helped one another survived better than groups whose members did not.)

If both behaviors exist within us, it is inaccurate to say that we need to learn to be generous. We already possess generosity. It's like a river that is always flowing within us. To enter the stream more readily, we need to peel away the dams to generosity that we have built up over our lives. We need to abandon the blocks we thought would keep us from feeling our own pain

The Attitudes of Radical Generosity

and the pain of others. We need to get rid of the attitudes that have reinforced our possessive aspects, so that the stream of generosity in our hearts can break free. The more we uncover the blocks, the more our generosity will gurgle and rush.

Giving Is Easy When We Go with the Grain

It doesn't matter how long we may have been stuck in a sense of our limitations. If we go into a darkened room and turn on the light, it doesn't matter if the room has been dark for a day, a week, or ten thousand years—we turn on the light and it is illumined. Once we contact our capacity for love and happiness . . . the light has been turned on.

—SHARON SALZBERG

The state of affairs in the world can often get you down. It's easy to become overwhelmed by all that needs fixing. It's equally easy to slip into despair, believing that since one person can't make a difference, it's not worth trying. However, there are many stories about people who decided to do something

that was important to them and who ended up having a huge impact. Think about the woman who started Mothers Against Drunk Drivers (MADD), for example, after her daughter was killed by a drunk driver. Since MADD's inception, drunk driving has declined every year. There's also four-year-old Isis Johnson, who asked her grandmother one day, "Can we send the chicken we have left to the children in Ethiopia?" With that question, she and her grandmother founded the Isis Johnson Foundation, which collects food and clothing for needy Louisianans.

The question for each of us is this: Where does your river of generosity naturally emerge? What is yours to give? Is it advice? Money? Time? Inspiring others to take action?

We each are born with a spark of life that is uniquely our own. We're here to find ways to express that spark, and when we can express it, giving is natural. It doesn't feel like work, because you are going with the grain of your being, not against it.

My husband, Don, expresses his spark through plants. He can work in the garden happily for hours. He's free with plant advice for anyone who asks and loves to give plants away. He'd be a natural for

helping to create a community garden, something he loves more than coaching little league sports. You also have a spark of life that, when tapped, gives you all kinds of energy and enthusiasm. The world needs that from you. If you aren't inclined to work with troubled adolescents, don't volunteer for it, even if the folks from your church are asking you to. If a particular activity doesn't speak to your soul, you'll be stuck in obligation and guilt, which are killers of the giving heart. Instead, find something you truly are enthusiastic about and express your giving in that way.

Every one of us needs opportunities to express our generosity, but they will be different for each of us. There is no one right way. By sticking with what feels natural to you, you will be more inclined to keep giving.

To Give Is to Live

What do we live for, if it is not to make life less difficult for each other?

—GEORGE ELIOT

I once read an Indian parable by Eknath Easwaran about a man who always lived the letter of the law and

was a model of respectability. When he died, he was sent to Chitragupta, the cosmic accountant who keeps the ledger on all human beings. Chitragupta looked up the man's name in the black book and found nothing. Nothing in the credit column, nothing in the debit column. Chitragupta didn't know what to do. He'd never encountered such a situation before. Here was a man who "had never helped anybody, never hurt anybody, never offended anybody, never loved anybody," writes Easwaran. "He couldn't be sent to heaven, but he couldn't be sent to hell either."

Chitragupta went to the god of creation, Brahma, figuring that since Brahma made the man, Brahma would know what to do. But Brahma, after studying all the heavenly statutes, couldn't figure out what to do with the guy either. "Take him to Krishna," he suggested. "Let him decide."

Krishna was determined to find a solution. He carefully examined the man's records again and saw, in almost invisible pencil, one entry in the credit column: "When six, gave two cents to a beggar." Now Krishna had the answer. "Give the man back his two cents and send him back to Earth to try again."

The Attitudes of Radical Generosity

Krishna's response shows the importance of giving. Under a strict accounting, the guy should have been let into heaven because he had one item in the credit column and no debits. The great Krishna, however, reasoned that one good deed is not enough, and the man was sent back to try again.

The nature of human life shows that we do both good and harm. It's impossible to go without helping or hurting others during the course of our lives, which is why the gods were stumped by a person who seemed to have done neither. We will, in the course of our lives, harm other beings, but until we have learned to give freely of ourselves, we have not truly learned how to live.

We Are Self-Renewing Systems

Life is constantly providing us with new funds, new resources, even when we are reduced to immobility. In life's ledger there is no such thing as frozen assets.

—HENRY MILLER

I have a friend whose father is a fisherman. Fishing has always been a hard vocation, and recently it has

been very difficult to make a living because of over-fishing. My friend's father is bitter and angry—at the government and at the other countries who have sent their huge boats just outside U.S. waters and depleted the fish population. He won't even entertain the possibility of doing something different with his life, even though he is quite talented with his hands. He just wants someone to fix the situation so he can go back to the way he was. Not coincidentally, he is one of the stingiest people I have ever met.

We often hold back on our generosity because we are afraid of running out—of money, of time, of ideas. This fear makes us think we need to cling to the way it was. We believe that "you can't teach an old dog new tricks," and we don't trust our capacity to renew ourselves or our ability to learn.

Living from a giving heart means knowing that each of us is a living system and that living systems are constantly learning and changing. With this view, how can you be afraid to give something away? You trust in your capacity to transform with the changing situation and to generate more, and you know that whatever you give will come back to you in another form.

The Attitudes of Radical Generosity

This is not an easy lesson for many of us. We have to let go of old mechanistic models of the world and trust in our capacity for regeneration. We are living in times where old ways of doing things are dying at a rapid rate and where we need to continually remake ourselves. My original work field—publishing—has changed dramatically over the past twenty years, and I have had to change as well. Chances are you have, too.

Even though I know that I am capable of learning, of growing and changing, I find myself sometimes sliding back into the old ways of thinking. Posting the quote by Henry Miller on my computer is one way I've found to bring myself back into my new ways of thinking. When I find myself scared and withholding, I also tell myself, "I'm intelligent and resourceful. I'm sure I can figure something out." When we trust in our capacity to generate and regenerate, we can be our generous selves more fully.

Generosity Comes in Many Forms

A gift consists not in what is done or given, but in the intention of the giver or doer.

—SENECA

In his spiritual autobiography, Gandhi talks about his shortcomings as a parent, particularly about not giving his sons enough of an academic education because he was more concerned with a moral one. His oldest son, he wrote, "has often given vent to his distress privately before me and publicly in the press; the other sons have generously forgiven the failure as unavoidable."

His words leaped out at me—I'd never thought of forgiveness as a generous act. Like any other generous act, though, it requires moving away from your self-focused perspective and making an overture to another. Forgiveness is particularly generous because it requires putting aside your own legitimate hurts in order to reestablish a new bond.

We tend to think of generosity in terms of money. Gandhi reminds us that there are many ways to be generous in our very being. We can give time, care, thanks, advice, and joy. We can give support or respectful distance. We can be generous listeners. We can be generous with our words, our touch, or our looks. We can be generous with our ideas, our creativity, or our knowledge. We can be generous with our possessions and our compassion. We can even be generous with our forgiveness.

My tenant Kathy jumps to mind when I think of the forms of generosity. She is so free with her enthusiasm, it is infectious. Bubbly, warm, and caring, she can jolly almost anyone out of a bad mood. She's always ready to volunteer for any project around the house. Need help moving rocks? Kathy volunteers. Need someone to go to the dump? She's ready to jump into action. Even though she embodies generosity to me, I doubt that she would characterize herself as generous, because we haven't been trained to think of our human qualities as reflecting generosity. Yet her essence, her very being, is a great gift to my family.

Where are you generous? Are you quick to forgive? Able to listen well? Know just when to offer a hug or a comforting hand on the shoulder? Full of ideas that you share freely? If our intention is to give from the abundance we feel, we are being generous, in whatever form we offer it. By narrowing our thinking about generosity, we deprive ourselves of myriad ways to live from our giving hearts, and we neglect to recognize the gifts we are offering on a daily basis by our very being.

We Can Make a Difference

*Even the most hard-nosed physicist is beginning to admit
that the flap of a butterfly's wings can change the weather
thousands of miles away. Everything we do matters.*

—GLORIA STEINEM

I was driving down the street one hot, dry, windy fall day, the most dangerous time of the year in California for fires. Looking uphill, I saw that a small fire had broken out in the tinder-dry grass between the street and a row of houses above me. Quickly I looked about for a phone and saw a small gas station up ahead. It was one of those tiny boxes with a person inside who takes your money and pushes a button to release the gas pump. I screeched up to the station and jumped out. No pay phone. I ran to the box, where a bored teenager sat inside.

"Excuse me," I said, "I've just seen a grassfire starting. Can I use your phone to call 911?"

"No," he said.

"Well, can you call 911 for me?" I asked.

"No," he responded. "It's not my problem."

Incredulous, I decided not to argue with him and raced off to find another phone.

Years ago, when the concept of self-esteem was all the rage, a professor in childhood development said to me, "You know, feeling good about yourself is important, but it's only a piece of what kids need. In addition to self-esteem, they need self-efficacy—the sense that they can take an action in the world and it will have an effect. So many kids, especially adolescents, feel that nothing they can do will make any difference, so why bother? They have never been taught that everything we do matters."

It was the first time I heard of self-efficacy, but it made a lot of sense to me. Like any other attribute, it becomes second nature if you practice it. If you call when you see a fire, the fire engines will come, and the fire will be put out quickly so that property and lives can be saved. Self-efficacy breeds action—if what I do can have an effect, somewhere, for someone, then I'm more inclined to do something.

While I know that there are people in the world like the kid who wouldn't call 911 for me, I think most of us have some sense of self-efficacy and some belief in our ability to have an effect. The complexity of the

problems that surround us makes it easy to lose faith in our efficacy or fall into despair.

When I begin to doubt my efficacy, I try two things. I sit a bit with my feelings of despair and really acknowledge the difficulty of what I am facing. Once I accept the complexity of the issue, I remind myself that while I cannot do everything, I can do something. Even though I will probably never know the effects of my action, it's worth trying. Maybe, for instance, my call to 911 that day saved someone's life. If not, it was worth doing anyway.

Whatever We Do, We Do for Ourselves

The gift is to the giver, and comes back most to him—it cannot fail.

—WALT WHITMAN

While writing this book, I heard the following story twice, which I took to be a definite sign that I was meant to use it here. It goes like this: There was a farmer who was the premier corn grower in his community. His corn was always sweeter and better than

The Attitudes of Radical Generosity

anyone else's, and it always won the blue ribbon at the county fair. At the end of the growing season, he would take his seed corn, the corn that would be sown the following spring, and gave a large portion of it to all the farmers in the area. "Why do you do that?" someone asked him. "Don't you want to keep the best corn for yourself?"

"I do it for myself," replied the farmer. "My corn will be cross-pollinated by bees and wind from the other fields, and if they have inferior corn, mine will soon become inferior as well."

That farmer really understood that the world is so interconnected that whatever we do for someone else we are also doing for ourselves. No action can be taken in isolation, because everything we do ripples out and has some kind of effect. The bad we do generates more bad—just think of all the places in the world caught up in religious or tribal feuds. Group A kills members of Group B, and the hatred generated from that act fuels Group B's killing of folks from Group A, and on and on down through the generations.

The ripple effect is true for good deeds as well, it's just less visible. Often, it is merely that the bad things

quit happening. The kid you help by becoming a Big Brother or Sister doesn't end up robbing you or raping your little sister. The person you tutor in reading is able to be a productive member of society rather than someone supported by welfare. The people you provided with a loan so they could set up a business exporting products from the rainforest in Brazil do not have to participate in killing the rainforest, a small step toward preserving our planet from destruction.

When we truly understand this interdependence, we also understand that whatever we do, we do for ourselves. As Dr. Martin Luther King, Jr., once said, "We may have all come on different ships, but we are all in the same boat now." And a mighty small boat it is.

Gratitude and Generosity Are Indivisible

As I express my gratitude, I become more aware of it. And the greater my awareness, the greater my need to express it. What happens here is a spiraling ascent, a process of growth in ever-expanding circles around a steady center.

—BROTHER DAVID STEINDL-RAST

The Attitudes of Radical Generosity

Years ago, my friend Grace got into a financial jam. She bought a one-bedroom condo in the boom years of the '80s, and then watched as the market for condos dropped like a rock. Then she was transferred to another state and couldn't get rid of it because she owed more on the mortgage than she could sell it for. She couldn't just walk away from it, because the bank could repossess the house she and her husband managed to buy despite the condo. So she rented it out, but the huge mortgage continued to be an albatross around her neck. Over the years, all of us close to Grace, including her friend Molly, have heard her express anxiety about the condo, especially whenever a tenant left.

Molly recently called up Grace to tell her that she and her husband had just made a killing because his Internet company went public, and that she was going to give Grace the money to pay off the mortgage on the condo. Grace was overwhelmed. "You can't do that," she said. "It's so much money." Molly replied, "I feel so grateful that my life has been so blessed. I just want to spread some of the blessings around. I've heard you complain about that condo for years. It would be give me great joy to alleviate your burden." Grace kept demurring, but Molly persisted, and finally

Radical Generosity

Grace accepted. As a consequence, Molly got to feel the delicious sensation of giving a huge gift to someone she loved.

Not only was Grace relieved of the burden of the condo, she also got to experience a sense of gratitude that spread to all aspects of her life. When telling me this story the other day, she said, "You know, I have been blessed with truly generous friends all my life. Molly ended up giving me more than I needed to pay off the loan. What I would really like to do now is to use the rest of the money to help my in-laws get out of debt."

Both Molly and Grace have entered the ever-expanding circle of openheartedness that comes from the interplay of generosity and gratitude. It doesn't matter where you enter the circle—in gratitude or with generosity. The more you experience one, the more the other enhances your life as well. You feel truly grateful, and from that fullness you offer something to someone else—an encouraging word or a helping hand. In return, you receive love, the feeling of connection, and a sense of satisfaction and fulfillment that continues to fuel your gratitude for the gifts of life you have received.

Few of us will ever be as extravagant in our giving as Molly, but that doesn't matter. This beautiful circle of giving and thankfulness occurs regardless of the size or the form of the gift.

We Are Both Generous and Withholding

Complete possession is proved only by giving. All you are unable to give possesses you.

—ANDRE GIDE

I have a friend who is one of the all-time great givers of emotional support. If you are upset, she is right there. She calls and will spend as long as you need talking about whatever's troubling you. She offers empathy and insight. She'll hold you in her awareness throughout the day and will check in ten times if that's what you need. When it comes to being a caring friend in a crisis, her generosity knows no bounds. Even though she's materially well off, I have never received a gift from her or been taken out to lunch. She's just not generous when it comes to material things.

We are all generous to greater or lesser degrees, and we are all generous in different realms. We've learned to be openhearted in some areas but not in others. It's good to take stock of just where and when we are and aren't generous. Once we become conscious of our habits, we have more freedom to change them, if we desire.

When I ask myself where I am generous, I realize that I offer my time and home to those I care about. I am also generous with my problem-solving abilities and my wisdom about how life seems to work. I also realize that I am especially stingy with money and sometimes stingy with praise, encouragement, or words of love, particularly with those I am close to.

My money stinginess makes sense to me. I am afraid of not having enough, so I hold back my generosity. I'm not afraid of running out of empathy or insight, so I give freely of those things. If I think deeply about Andre Gide's quote, I see that my stinginess with money is a problem. In a certain sense, money does possess me. I spend a great deal of time worrying about how to get it and how to keep it, while the people I know who are generous with money, regardless of how much they have, are not obsessed by it.

The Attitudes of Radical Generosity

My stinginess with verbal support comes, I think, from my fear that I will have to give everything in a relationship while the other person does nothing. The problem here is that my verbal stinginess virtually ensures that the other person will not want to give me the love and nurturing I want. Love is a cycle that grows in a mutual atmosphere of freely given and received care and concern.

Where are you generous and where are you stingy? Ask yourself, and then see what the answers reveal. You don't have to change the way you are, but a little insight might offer some new perspectives.

We Can Unblock Our Giving

In the long run, we get no more than we have been willing to risk giving.

—SHELDON KOPP

A few years ago, I was in the produce market and, in the middle of the lettuce aisle, saw a large bin of sweet peas for sale. They are one of my favorite flowers, so I picked a bunch and held them up to my nose. A woman passing by commented on how beautiful they

were and asked me how much they cost. "Two dollars," I proclaimed. "Would you like a bunch?'" "Oh," she said, hesitating, "I'd better not. I'm watching my budget." She then turned and walked away. How sad, I thought, she obviously wanted them but wasn't able to spend the two dollars. So I picked out a bunch, went to the checkout stand, paid for them, and then found her in a different aisle. "Here," I said, "I want you to have these." She wouldn't take them, and I left feeling frustrated and embarrassed. I had wanted to give someone a treat, but my giving was blocked. I've never tried to do such a thing again.

We all have reasons why we hold ourselves back from giving. Perhaps we tried in the past and were unsuccessful, so we've learned to limit that impulse. As a child, perhaps we got in trouble for giving our toys away to friends or got burned out in young adulthood because of a volunteer position we took on. Maybe we're angry that we haven't gotten what we think we deserve in life, so we resent the thought of anyone else having something. Perhaps we're so busy we can't even see our own needs, much less anyone else's. We could also hold certain self-protecting ideas, like "It's a

dog-eat-dog world," because we are covering up some deep hurt we experienced when young, one that now keeps us from reaching out.

These reasons deserve some examination, because they are the bricks in the dam that is holding back the flow of giving in your life. As long as they remain as solid and hard as they are now, you will limit the experience of joy that giving can bring to you.

I'm not suggesting that you dynamite the dam. These bricks have served some good purpose for you. They have protected you from some hurt that you had no other way to deal with at the time. All I'm suggesting is that you reexamine them now and determine whether they are still necessary. The first step is "seeing clearly how we hold back, how we pull away, how we shut down, how we close off, and then learning how to open," as Buddhist teacher Pema Chödrön puts it.

Why do you hold yourself back from giving as much as you can? Gently ask the question and gently receive the answer. The most important place to express your generosity in this moment is toward yourself and for all you have endured that has caused your heart to close in the first place.

You Can't Say Yes
if You Can't Say No

*We need to respectfully pay attention to ourselves, tuning
in when the little voice inside wants to say "no."*

—SUE PATTON THOELE

My friend Monica just spent some time at a Zen retreat
center, where she was asked to correspond with a male
prisoner who had written looking for a Buddhist pen
pal. She didn't want to but felt she should, so she
agreed to write. She did say that she would prefer writing to a woman but was told that there were no women
in the pile.

It's been a month now. Every day she says she
should write that letter, and every day she doesn't.
Every day she feels guilty—a "good" person would
have already written the letter—and feels resentful
that she was roped into the situation in the first place.

Monica's problem is familiar to many of us, particularly women: She can't say no. As I told my husband when I first met him, if you can't say no, you
can't say yes. That's because in order to truly say yes to

something, it has to be wholehearted. You have to really mean it, and you can't really mean it if you don't feel free to say no, especially if that's what is true for you.

People who have trouble saying no take on too much and end up bitter and burned out. They are the women who bake the cookies for every classroom event, drive all the kids in the neighborhood to the movies every weekend, singlehandedly take on the new project at work—all while tending to their dying parent. At the very least, they are exhausted, but most likely they are prone to feelings of martyrdom; they're holding up the whole world while the rest of us are just loafing around. Maybe they have twenty-five people angry with them because they couldn't possibly meet all their commitments, and they feel victimized by the other people's anger; after all, they are trying so hard and doing so much!

This kind of giving is not giving at all. It is a compulsion that usually comes from a lack of self-worth. They are so afraid of the disapproval of the person making the request that they must say yes. As a result, they have never experienced true generosity,

which comes from an overflow of a sense of caring not compulsion.

Even if we don't suffer from low self-esteem, it can be hard to disappoint someone who is making a direct request of us. But unless we begin to truly listen for our "nos," our "yeses," like Monica's, will be half-hearted at best and a true burden at worst.

True Giving Means Letting Go of Control

Blessed are those who can give without remembering.

—ELIZABETH BIBESCO

I have a friend whose father is so wealthy he has established a trust fund for his children that will begin doling out money after he dies. It doesn't matter to him that his children are already in their fifties and could use the money now—to send their kids to college, to help support an ill wife. Nor does it matter to him that they are all quite capable of managing any money they would receive after his death. He wants to control how much, when, and how they get the money, even after he is dead.

My friend's situation is not unique. I know three other people with parents so committed to control that they hold on even from the grave. Some folks would argue that since the money is theirs, they have a right to say how and when it is used. They may have a point, but don't confuse this outlook with generosity. This approach is simply purchasing something with your money—you behave like this, and I will give you that—or expressing your disapproval—you haven't lived the way I want, so I will not let you have a say.

True giving says, "Here, take this and do what you think you should with it. I give you freedom. I let go of whatever I think should happen and allow you to do what you think is right." True generosity follows the pattern of nature—the seed lets go of its identity in order for the tree to sprout; the caterpillar lets go of its old form in order to become a butterfly. For the new to emerge, the old generously lets go of form and identity. It doesn't try to cling to itself but graciously gives way.

By clinging, you never get to experience the joy that comes with true giving. I was reminded of that the other day by a friend in her seventies who gave $5,000 to her kids when an annuity of hers came due. "It's

more fun to give it," she said, "than it was to get it." So true. The fun comes in giving the gift and watching the other person delightedly receive it. When we put conditions on our giving, we miss out on that whole-hearted receiving. My friend's father may end up "giving" his children millions, but he will never receive their thanks, because his stingy conditions preclude any feelings of gratitude.

If You Give, You Will Be Provided For

If you help others you will be helped, perhaps tomorrow, perhaps in one hundred years, but you will be helped. Nature must pay off the debt.... It is a mathematical law and all life is mathematics.

—GURDJIEFF

Long before managed care, my father was a small-town family doctor, the old-fashioned kind who made house calls, birthed babies, and comforted the dying when they were beyond medical help. Everyone in town knew him and assumed we were rich because he was a doctor. My father, who grew up in the slums of

Boston, was never rich, because he kept his fees low and gave away a lot of care for free.

This was when all the talk was about the coming of socialized medicine. My father didn't believe in it, he said, because he thought every doctor should volunteer to see a percentage of patients for free. If every doctor did, then everyone would have adequate care (and, as a side benefit, all the reimbursement paperwork would be eliminated). When he retired, I helped him close his office. I was supposed to send out final bills, but I just listened to him tell me why so-and-so could not pay and should not be billed. He knew everyone's story.

When I asked him why he wasn't more concerned about money, he said that, given his background, he felt very rich and didn't need any more than he had, and that it was his privilege to give his medical gift to as many people as possible. Our family may never have been affluent, but we certainly had all we needed. When my father died, twenty years after retirement, the church was packed with former patients, nurses, and doctors who came to say thanks and good-bye to a man with a big heart.

My father was a person who had his priorities straight. So many of us think that our security

lies in accumulating a big wad of cash, and we make that the focus of our lives. Even if we succeed in our stockpiling, stock markets can crash and banks can fail. Our true safety comes in offering our gifts to the world and trusting that by doing what we love, we will be provided for in return. We may not have the best car, the biggest house, or the yacht in the harbor. We will have the immense satisfaction that comes from using our gifts to their fullest, something no amount of money can buy. By giving our best self to the world, we will be creating a strong network of loving friends, family, and neighbors who will be there for us, no matter what happens.

Let Go of the Ledger Sheet

You have not lived a perfect day, even though you have earned your money, unless you have done something for someone who will never be able to repay you.

—RUTH SMELTZER

I can't say I have measured up to Ruth Smeltzer's yardstick for a perfect day, because there are many, many days that I have not done something for someone else.

The Attitudes of Radical Generosity

Despite her high standard, this quote points to something that is crucial to understand about giving: In a sense, the things we do for one another can never be repaid, so when it comes to living from a giving heart, we have to forget the ledger sheet.

Here's what I mean by ledger sheet. Years ago, my husband and I were friends with another couple. It was more of a social friendship than anything else; my husband worked with her husband. She was very proper, and the rules of society dictated that if you were invited to dinner at their house, you must then invite them to yours. You would not be invited back to their house—even if they wished to see you—until you had fulfilled your obligation to feed them.

That's the ledger sheet—you do this, and I will repay you by doing that. Somewhere in the back of our minds, we keep track of our giving and receiving to make sure it comes out even. You give me a present worth a hundred dollars, and I must give something of equal value. In this system, everything, including ourselves, is a commodity, and we must exchange equally, or one of us is going to feel ripped off.

This ledger view implies that there is not enough to go around, so things must be very carefully doled

out and tracked. Not only is this exhausting, it completely squashes genuine caring, because it fails to take into account the circumstances of one another's lives. What if you don't have a home that can host a dinner party or enough money to take me out to eat? I would never see you. Because I have more money than you, I have to be careful not to give you anything that you can't repay.

Fundamentally, the ledger sheet just doesn't work. How can your husband, for instance, repay you for helping raise his children as a stepparent? Raising kids is an act of love, pure and simple, that has to be given with no strings attached. Otherwise, the burden of guilt will be so heavy on him that he will have to minimize your contribution to feel okay about himself. You will receive no appreciation and the love between you will shrivel up. With the ledger sheet, our caring is always pinched. We have to be afraid—of being "taken advantage of." The person on the receiving end better figure out how to pay up, or they will feel guilty and have to deflect your giving in order to feel equal again.

There's a way to give without the ledger sheet, a way that says, "I feel loving toward you, and I want to express that to the level I feel like. Period. I express my

The Attitudes of Radical Generosity

caring and you express yours." In the case of the dinner party problem, if I want to see you, let's eat at my house every time. You'll figure out a way to be generous, too—perhaps by bringing a great bottle of wine or flowers or offering to babysit my child.

When we give up the ledger sheet and are truly giving what we want to, there's no danger of feeling ripped off. We want to buy her the wreath because we think it will make her happy, and we want her to know we love her—not because we want something in return.

I have been working on giving up the ledger sheet over the past few years, and I've been fairly successful. Holidays are my downfall, because they come with an expectation of a gift exchange, so I fall into the trap of giving in order to get. If I give a present to someone and don't get one in return, I notice that I feel bad. If I give a gift spontaneously at another time of the year, I feel great. The commercialized gift-giving that accompanies our holidays only reinforces the ledger sheet idea.

Radical Generosity

You Never Know What the Effects of Your Actions Will Be

"Let me light the lamp," says the star,
"And never debate if it will help to remove the darkness."

—RABINDRANATH TAGORE

My mother has a niece whom she loves very much. This niece has four sons and a life that doesn't allow for many extras. So when the boys were young, my mother, who lives on Cape Cod, used to invite them down each summer for a vacation. One year, she decided to pay for sailing lessons for Mike, one of the sons who expressed interest in learning to sail. She knew her niece couldn't afford it on her own. Mike is now in his twenties, and he makes a living sailing around the world. Inadvertently, my mother helped Mike discover his passion and his profession!

My mother's story reminded me that we can never know what the effects of our actions will be. All we can do is live from our hearts and trust that the goodness we do will ripple out into the world. We can't get too attached to a particular outcome. By paying for the

sailing lessons, my mother wasn't trying to turn Mike into a sailor, she just was offering him a chance to sail.

Buddhist teacher Jack Kornfield has a story about the problems with having strings attached to our giving. Kornfield was a young monk in Asia, where beggars abound. He would go back and forth to the temple to meditate, passing the beggars every day. Finally, he was about to leave the area and, filled with compassion, he decided to take what money he could afford, have it changed into many bills of small denominations, and, looking each person in the eyes and bowing respectfully, hand over the money. It was to be an offering of respect as well as money, done mindfully to each person.

He walked up to the first beggar and all went according to plan. He looked deeply into his eyes, he bowed, he carefully handed over the money. As soon as the other beggars saw the money, they immediately began to mob him. All sense of ceremony was lost as they scrambled for the cash. He ended up throwing all the money into the air and running like hell!

We give because we want to give. We don't give so it will turn out a certain way, or because we will get thanked. We give because we want to experience the

joy that comes from offering whatever it is that is ours to offer. In the words of T. S. Eliot, "For us, there is only the trying. The rest is not our business."

All True Giving Is Loving

Love has nothing to do with what you are expecting to get—only what you are expecting to give.

—KATHERINE HEPBURN

I heard a great story recently about a young man who, fired up with religious teachings on compassion and generosity, decided to make a bunch of peanut butter and jelly sandwiches so he could give them away to homeless people in his neighborhood. He couldn't give away even one sandwich. Nobody wanted what he had to offer. So he thought to himself, "This giving thing is more complicated than I thought. If I really want to be helpful, maybe I should find out what these people want."

The next day, he went out empty-handed. All he did was say hello to a few people and strike up a conversation about the weather. The next day, he again spoke to the same people, this time asking a bit

about how they were doing. This went on for a while, until he discovered that what they really wanted was something sweet—sandwiches were the main fare at the homeless shelters. He began to make brownies, incredible, wonderful brownies, and offer those along with conversation.

This young man discovered that to truly give, you must know what is wanted. To know that, you must form a relationship with the other—you have to love them. Love is merely the willingness to know the other person as he or she truly is, and then offering yourself as you truly are. This man was willing to drop all expectations of how he thought homeless people should be—that a hungry person should want a peanut butter sandwich or even that a hungry person should be grateful for anything—to discover who they actually were and then offer what he could of who he was. That's as wonderful an act of love as any other I know of.

In love, we look outside ourselves at the other and want the best for them. In love, we feel our hearts swell as we seek to bring happiness or peace or comfort to the other. What is true giving except these very things?

Radical Generosity

In order to truly give, we need to actually see the people we are reaching out to. We need to understand that, just like us, they want to be happy. We need to recognize that, just like us, they are suffering. And from this awareness, our loving compassion is born.

When we remember that giving is loving, we are able to be more accurate in our giving. When we experience giving as loving, we feel the joy that our generous actions can bring.

Think Positive!

Gladness is akin to goodness. The world needs all the help you can give by way of cheerful, optimistic, inspiring thought and personal example.

—GRENVILLE KLEISER

My business partner, Will, and I lived together for fourteen years. Whenever we got into a hard place with one another, and I complained about our relationship to my friend Daphne, she would always ask me why I stayed with him. The question wasn't meant as criticism of my choice but was her way to remind me of the good things about our relationship. I would

The Attitudes of Radical Generosity

79

always give the same answer: "Because he is cheerful every single day." Since I find it easy to sink down into depression, his upbeat temperament was a true joy to be around. Eventually, I decided I wanted to cultivate my own positiveness instead of being dependent on someone else to provide it. While I don't pretend to be as practiced at it as a lifelong optimist, I'm trying.

My efforts in this direction are the most generous thing I can do for those around me. Cynicism, alienation, and disaffection abound in our society. It's not cool to be hopeful, to be cheerful, to be optimistic, or to care too much.

Such cynicism is a cover. We've been hurt somewhere along the line and want to make sure we're not hurt again. Giving up hope and caring, we reason, will protect us from further pain. Sealed off in our bubble of misery, however, we are continually injured by our old hurt. Have you ever met a pessimist who was happy and not just content in his or her misery? Pessimists are too busy protecting themselves from pain to feel anything but pain. Only by risking happiness and hoping, even trusting, in a good outcome do we have any hope of rising out of our personal misery.

This is true with our approach to the external world. Instead of being immobilized by our cynicism, which allows for no movement at all and increases the possibility of bad things happening, we should strive for optimism and hope for the best. Optimism, even learned optimism like mine, creates the possibility of movement and of discovering solutions. Hope and cheerfulness create the energy that opens us to the possible future and the potentially good outcome. Adopting a can-do attitude is the most generous thing we can do right now. The more of us who adopt it, the more the force of positive change will be unleashed in the world. Now that's a gift that's worth giving!

Strive for Balance

It is better to give and receive.

—BERNARD GUNTHER

About a year ago, two authors of mine, a couple, offered to let me use their house in Hawaii. "Thank you," I said politely, "I can't get over there now, but I appreciate the offer." Inside, I was feeling terribly uncomfortable. It was such a generous offer, and I

didn't know them very well; how could I possibly take them up on it? I wondered if they really meant it.

Several months later, they repeated the offer, with the same results. I deflected their kindness and felt embarrassed and confused. Then I ran into them again, and we went through the same process. As I walked away, something changed in me. It was partly because I had just read something about Buddha and Jesus never refusing anyone who asked them something three times. Mostly, it was that I was beginning to think about generosity and wanted to examine what was going on more closely.

I realized that they must really mean it—after all, they did offer three times. I understood that they had appreciated what I had done for them as an editor and wanted to demonstrate their gratitude. By constantly refusing, I was not allowing them to express their thanks to me.

I had a part in this exchange, too. Even though it's hard for me to be on the receiving end in general, I felt unworthy to receive such a generous gesture. Taking in the idea that someone wanted to do something so nice for me was painful, and that was standing in my way of getting to have a wonderful experience.

Radical Generosity

I came to understand that receiving is as important as giving, otherwise no gift would ever find its home. The receiver has an important part in the process. It takes grace to say, "Yes, I would love that," or "That would be wonderful, thank you." It implies that you believe you are worth getting whatever it is that is being offered. I was used to being in the position of "giver." That felt comfortable and safe to me. I could give and feel good about myself in the giving. But feeling good in the receiving was a whole new frontier. I decided to call the couple up and say yes. I went and had a marvelous time in their beautiful retreat. While I must admit it still felt a bit awkward, I remembered that all new behavior feels awkward, because we haven't practiced it much.

Are you off-balance as well? Is it easy for you to give but not to receive? Are you comfortable receiving and withhold in your giving? Being generous is a two-sided process, and experiencing both sides is vital to our well-being and growth. Without giving, we become cut off from the human family; without receiving, we are in danger of becoming burned-out, resentful wrecks.

It's Both an Inside
and Outside Job

There is a pervasive form of contemporary violence to which the idealist ... most easily succumbs: ... activism and overwork. ... To allow oneself to be carried away by a multitude of conflicting concerns, to surrender to too many demands, to commit oneself to too many people, to want to help everyone in everything, is to succumb to violence. The frenzy ... kills the root of inner wisdom which makes work fruitful.

—THOMAS MERTON

When I was in my twenties, I was, like so many others in the late '60s and early '70s, convinced that I could change the world merely through the force of my desire for it to change. I lived in a large commune dedicated to social and political change, and the twenty of us who lived there spent every waking moment rushing to meetings, holding events, picketing, and marching. We may have screamed for peace and bullied others to be more tolerant and understanding, but we felt good

about ourselves. At least we were giving—unlike all those unfeeling, lazy, middle-class slobs around us.

Inside myself, however, something felt profoundly wrong. The problem, it seemed to me, was not just with the "system" but with the way we were relating to it. It didn't seem right to be so angry or so violent. We never had time to look at ourselves, even if we had wanted to, though. We were too busy.

Over time, like so many other people, I drifted away from activism. Not because I had lost my ideals but because I didn't know how to actualize them. I spent time on myself; I helped raise a family. I always felt bad that I wasn't giving to the world in the way I thought I should. How could I make a difference, though? My previous attempt had been so useless.

One day, I heard Vietnamese monk Thich Nhat Hanh speak of the peace activists he had met in the United States. "They want peace, but they aren't peaceful. To have peace, you must be peace." I realized that my fellow activists and I had been busy trying to create peace around us, but we were anything but peaceful inside.

The Attitudes of Radical Generosity

With this realization, I really came to see that true giving has two aspects. One is internal, the cultivation of wisdom within yourself so that your gift is both appropriate and skillfully offered. The other is external, the actual proffering of time, money, skills, perspective, or commitment. Like the balance needed between giving and receiving, the inside and outside components of giving need to be in balance as well. If we just "work on ourselves," the wisdom we cultivate goes unused, like a farmer who refuses to harvest his crop. If we spend all our time running around trying to save the world, as Thomas Merton points out, we never develop—or we lose track of—the inner qualities that allow our generosity to be fruitful. Only in stillness can such qualities of character be born, and only in living them out can they ever become actualized.

To grow our giving hearts, we need to engage in a beautiful dance of reaching out and then turning in, action and reflection, movement and stillness. The cultivation of both our inner and outer lives is where true generosity resides.

We Are God's Hands in the World

God's work must truly be our own.

—JOHN F. KENNEDY, IN HIS
INAUGURAL ADDRESS

There is a wonderful Sufi teaching story about a spiritual seeker who was praying outside. As he prayed, he noticed a constant stream of beggars, people crippled in body and mind or in spirit and heart, go past him. He looked at this mass of suffering humanity and, lifting his voice to God, cried, "Great God, how is it that a loving creator can see such things and yet do nothing about them?"

Then, out of the long silence, came the voice of God, saying, "I did do something. I made you."

That story never fails to inspire me, no matter how many times I read it. The world is full of misery and full of great physical and emotional hardships. Sometimes I think about what humans endure—starvation, war, the death of loved ones, abuse, torture—and am amazed that life goes on at all. All the great spiritual traditions address the fact of human suffering, and each of us has to somehow wrap her mind around it, too.

The Attitudes of Radical Generosity

Life is more than suffering. It also contains joy, laughter, and renewal. Life contains peace, beauty, and contentment. It contains human beings with the consciousness to be aware of suffering and who want to do something about it. We are God's hands, voice, and eyes on Earth. Because we are aware of suffering, we are also capable of compassion and empathy. Through our compassion, we can reach out to offer our arms to a person who needs a hug or their burden carried, if only for a little while. We can offer a kind or encouraging word or a look that says, "I see what you are going through. Is there anything I can do to help?"

When we act in empathy and compassion, we make God's love incarnate. We become, as the Christian hymn says, like "angels descending, bring from above, echoes of mercy, whispers of love."

God has no hands but ours. How will you use yours?

Radical Generosity

CHAPTER 4

The Practices of Radical Generosity

One thing I realized after practicing radical generosity is that everyone has something going on that you just can't appreciate, that you can't see, that holds them back at times. We all have our bad days. Now, when someone comes at me with anger, frustration , judgement, or know-it-all-ness, instead of getting combative or "reacting," I take a deep breath, smile inside, and give a radically generous response.

—MICHELLE SAVOY, SHEEO ACTIVATOR

This section offers practices we can use to expand our experience of giving. We go beyond our feelings of openheartedness to specific behaviors that will bring that feeling alive in the world. The ultimate goal is expressing our feelings of generosity in a variety of ways that bring joy to ourselves and others. The more we do, the more we will experience firsthand the ultimate grace of the giving heart—happiness, contentment, and the enlargement of the soul that comes when we live from, in the words of Sharon Salzberg, "a heart as wide as the world."

Become More Aware of Your Generosity

There is nothing forced or self-disciplined about [generosity]. . . . [A generous person] goes out of his way, not because his parents taught him that's how good [people] behave, but because he has chosen to be alert to the circumstances in which he can be supportive.

—TIBOR R. MACHAN

My friend Dawna Markova is the most generous person I know. Before starting this book, the first thing I did was to talk to her. I asked her about her own generosity—where she thought it came from and what her relationship to it was. Normally a font of wisdom on every subject, she was, at first, uncharacteristically silent. Finally she said, "I don't know what to say. It's such a value to me, such a part of my training, that it's

like asking a fish to describe water." She went on to be her usual brilliant self on the subject, but that initial hesitation stuck with me.

There have been several studies done on kidney donors to determine what makes someone willing to give a part of their own body to another person. In almost every single case, the donor felt it was no big deal. It didn't seem like a sacrifice, or something that had to be mulled over. Someone was in need, and the donor was glad to be able to respond.

In his book *Generosity*, Tibor Machan claims generosity is a virtue we can choose to cultivate or not, but that once we choose to cultivate it, it becomes invisible to us. When we operate from our sense of generosity, we don't have to think about whether we're going to give something. We just do. What differentiates generosity from charity, he claims, is its lack of deliberation. With charity, we have a sense that we should give something to another person or a cause because it is the right thing to do. When we operate from generosity, we don't even think about right or wrong. We just give as a matter of course.

The ways we are generous are invisible to us because they are a natural part of our being. Without

The Practices of Radical Generosity

hesitating, we'll drive an extra hour out of our way to pick up Grandma, or we'll schedule time to speak to a friend's daughter who is thinking about a career in our field. No matter how busy we are, we'll call a friend who has just suffered a loss. It's wonderful to have generous impulses, but the problem with the invisibility of your generosity is that you can have all kinds of false perceptions about your ability to give. All of the wonderful things you give as a matter of course may be completely off your radar screen. In my case, I think of myself as someone who is stingy with money. After reading about the kidney donors, though, I remembered that I lent my sister a pretty big sum so she'd have enough for a down payment to buy a house. Despite my money fears, giving to my sister was such an "of course" that my act didn't even register on my internal self-monitor.

Take a few moments to remind yourself of the ways you have been generous in the past and are being so now. Bring all the ways you are giving into the light of your awareness and celebrate them.

Radical Generosity

Look at Your Gifts

What are the gifts that we've been given? To deny that we are gifted is, perhaps, to indulge in false humility, which allows us to shirk responsibility for the gift. But the gift is a sacred trust.... It asks that we develop it. And it asks that we pass it on.

—DEENA METZGER

I was an editor for twenty-two years. One day, I was meeting with a well-known writer for the first time. She asked me something—perhaps how I could help her—and part of what I said was, "Well, I'm really good at looking at something and knowing what goes where, and what else might be needed. It's just a gift I have of being able to see the whole and the parts at the same time." She hired me on the spot, not only, she said, because I could help her but also because she sees herself as very insecure, and it was a great gift to her that I was so able matter-of-factly to acknowledge my ability.

Stating what I'm good at comes easily to me. Perhaps because in some way I don't feel I "own"

my talents. They have been given to me, and it is my sacred duty to cultivate them and my sacred honor to pass them on. I have been given the ability to analyze, and it is my both my obligation and my delight to offer that to the world, first as an editor and now as a thinking partner/coach/mentor to entrepreneurs and executives around the world.

Before we can offer our gifts, we need to know what they are, which can be difficult for many people, especially women. We are taught to be modest, to downplay our strengths, and to focus on our faults. It begins in childhood when everyone around us at school and at home is fixated on what we are doing wrong instead of what's right about us. As a consequence, we grow up unaware of the very precious gifts that have been given to us to use.

To begin to know who we are and what we are here to offer, we need to look at what we've already given in our lives and what we've received. From there, we can begin to create a more accurate picture of where our gifts are and what our purpose here on Earth might be.

Here's an exercise to acknowledge your talents from Deena Metzger's wonderful book *Writing for Your Life*: Make two lists, one of gifts you've given and one of gifts you've received. After you are done, look at both of these lists as if you just found them on the street corner and you know nothing else about the person who wrote them. Then, writes Metzger, "develop a portrait of the person who emerges from this series of exchanges by examining the nature of the lists, the kinds and qualities of the gifts given and received, and their relationship to one another. . . . Who is this person?"

Set Your Intention

A hundred times every day I remind myself that my inner and outer life depends on the labors of other men, living and dead, and that I must exert myself in order to give in the measure as I have received and am still receiving.

—ALBERT EINSTEIN

It's so easy to get busy in our own lives, to shut down our awareness and see only what needs to be done in

The Practices of Radical Generosity

front of us instead of anyone or anything else. I often find myself bustling around, so focused on getting my list done that I don't even take time to say hello to people around me. Sometimes I find myself walking out the door when someone is still speaking to me! If they did need something of me, how would I know? I'm moving too fast for it to even register.

Because my life is so full and so speeded up, I find it helpful to take a moment when I wake up to set my intention to be helpful to others that day. The phrase I say is very simple—"May I be of use"—but it has profound effects. It focuses me on what is most important and reminds me that meeting the deadline, for example, is important, but not as important as being caring to those I meet throughout the day. Setting this intention makes it more likely that when I do get speedy and unconscious of those around me, I will take a deep breath and look around at those with whom I am sharing this life.

This is what Einstein means. We will get busy and self-involved and forget to notice anything but ourselves. Even though we will forget every single day, if we set our intention, we create a base to go back to.

Radical Generosity

We can begin to notice when we are forgetting and return to our resolution to live by our giving heart. Give it a try.

Tomorrow, when you wake up, ask to be of use as you go through your day. It needs to be in your own words, from your heart. Here are some examples: "May I make a difference in the world today." "May I be of service to one person." "May I notice myself and others." "May I give the gift that only I can give." Notice how that reverberates throughout the day. If you prefer, you can say this beautiful Buddhist verse:

> May I become at all times, both now and
>   forever
> A protector for those without protection
> A guide for those who have lost their way
> A ship for those with oceans to cross
> A sanctuary for those in danger
> A lamp for those without light
> A place of refuge for those who lack shelter
> And a servant to all in need

The Practices of Radical Generosity

Begin Somewhere

What one does is what counts and not what one had the intention of doing.

—PABLO PICASSO

I don't know about you, but I am full of good intentions. I intend to do yoga, meditate every morning, and create Ana's adoption scrapbook. Tomorrow. Somehow tomorrow never comes, or, more accurately, tomorrow comes, but I am stuck in the same ruts and routines as today, so my good intentions go nowhere. Like any new behavior, we have to stop talking about it and begin to do it. Somewhere, somehow—but where and how?

As an editor, I had the privilege of working with Jackie Waldman, the author of *The Courage to Give: Inspiring Stories of People Who Triumphed over Tragedy to Make a Difference in the World.* It's a series of profiles of people who have suffered great physical or emotional difficulties and healed themselves by reaching out to help others. It's partly Jackie's story, too—she has multiple sclerosis, and she has found that the more she gives to others, the better she feels physically and emotionally. Her discovery amazed her, and in her desire to

see whether this happened to other people as well, she found many people for whom this was true. Her book, and its follow-up companion, *Teens with the Courage to Give*, provide substance to Edwin Markham's words that "all that we send into the lives of others comes back into our own."

As a result of her books, Jackie has become a national spokesperson for the transformative power of volunteerism. I spoke to her recently about giving, and she said that virtually everyone she meets wants to be helpful to others, but many of us don't know where to start. "I've learned in these situations," she said, "to ask people three questions. That's all it takes." Here are Jackie's questions. Try them today.

---

(1) What do you love to do? (2) To whom do you feel drawn to lend a hand? (3) Is there something that speaks to your heart? Ask yourself these questions and listen deeply to the answers. Then, armed with the information from your heart, you can try logging onto *volunteermatch .org*, plug in your responses, and find all kinds of choices right in your own backyard.

The Practices of Radical Generosity

Share What You Love

*Don't worry about what the world wants from you,
worry about what makes you come more alive.
Because what the world really needs are people who
are more alive.*

—LAWRENCE LA SHAN

My friend Andy is a wonderful bodyworker. Among other things, he does Touch For Health, which is a system for finding out what substances, like vitamins and minerals, your body needs. In the ten years I have known him, he's offered his knowledge to me and many other people, as well as taught the system to several people. I've never seen him charge one penny. Helping people is something that makes him come alive, and sharing it makes him feel good. My husband, Don, has an intuitive gift for picking stocks and has made a lot of money at it. Recently he has begun to email stock suggestions to friends, not because he wants a commission but because it feels good to be using his talent, and he wants to share it with others.

We all have things we love to do that make us come alive. I love to edit. Although I do it to make a living, I also give it away for "free" to friends who want me to look at a proposal they're writing, a novel they're penning, or a letter they're sending. Editing makes me feel more alive, and I am grateful for the chance to feel that exhilaration whenever the opportunity presents itself. It's similar to a racehorse wanting to run as fast as it can or a great skier wanting to swoop down the mountain. It just feels good to use your abilities to the utmost. Sharing that good feeling with someone else by imparting your knowledge is just icing on the cake.

Think about what you love to do. List a few items to yourself: I love to make quilts; I enjoy fixing cars; I love archeology. Imagine that the things you love are jewels that you keep locked up tight in a jewelry box instead of taking them out and wearing them. By keeping them locked up, you miss out on the enjoyment of wearing them and using them, and other people miss out on seeing them and maybe trying them on. Try wearing that diamond or displaying that emerald.

> Think of one thing you could do for others by doing what you love. Get a group together to make crib quilts for hospitalized babies. Teach some inner city kid to fix a car. Take a group out on an archeological trip around your town. Start with what you love and the intention to share it, and the rest will be easy.

Cultivate Compassion

The worse people act, the greater is their need for healing.

—A COURSE IN MIRACLES

I was walking in the crosswalk on a busy street in San Francisco this past Christmas, and a dapper older gentleman, dressed to the nines with a hat and a cane, was walking down the street toward me. I was just about to reach the curb when a taxi turning right on the red light almost plowed into me. I stopped to make sure it wouldn't hit me, and then, when I knew that the taxi driver had seen me, I continued walking. As I did, the old man suddenly blurted out, "Wake up you *******
*****." I walked a couple more steps and then turned

around, trying to verify that he had been addressing his obscenities to me. Seeing me turn, he said, "Yes, I mean you, you ******* *****."

I was shocked. I had done nothing to provoke him; he was quite far from me, so I hadn't cut him off or slowed him down. As the shock wore off, I remembered the quote from *A Course in Miracles* and felt great compassion. What must have happened to this man in his life that he felt the need to say such a thing to me?

This realization has come in handy many other times—when someone is verbally attacking me or when I learn about back-stabbing comments someone has made. If I can see their need for healing instead of shutting down, running, or attacking, I can engage my compassion. I can offer silent wishes that they be healed once I recognize that they must be in some kind of pain to behave in such a hurting way. Even when I find myself behaving in a less than stellar way, I acknowledge my need for healing and apologize.

Increasing my compassion allows me to stay connected to my heart and lets me release the full power of my generosity. Disconnecting from our compassion means that there is no possibility we can give to others.

The Practices of Radical Generosity

Sealed off from our loving nature, we can't see whatever need might be presenting itself.

Remaining compassionate is not easy, particularly when we are under attack. In her column in the *Shambhala Sun*, therapist Karen Kissel Wegela offers this strategy, called the Difficult Person (DP) exercise. It's a truly radically generous act. As Wegela notes, people who do this exercise often discover "that what the DP wanted was something much simpler than what we had thought. Often it is easy for us to imagine giving it to them, and we find we become more tender." At the very least, this exercise makes it easier for us to understand their pain and why they might be treating us poorly. That discovery is enough to open our hearts.

Sit quietly alone for a few minutes. Then, imagine that a Difficult Person (DP) is sitting across from you at eye level. For a few minutes, bring this person into as much vivid detail as you can. Now imagine that you are the DP. Notice what is it like to be in his or her body. How old are you? Are you in pain? What emotions are you feeling? In the role of the DP, look across at you. What do you want from this person who is having such a hard time with you? Imagine that you, the DP, actually got what you needed from this other person. What would it feel like to have received it?

Become yourself again and look at the DP. How does it feel to have given him or her what was needed? Is it possible for you to really do this?

The Practices of Radical Generosity

Surprise Someone

Giving brings happiness at every stage of its expression.
We experience joy in forming the intention to be generous;
we experience joy in the actual act of giving something;
and we experience joy in remembering the fact that we
have given.

—BUDDHA

Elizabeth had planned a surprise weekend ski trip for her husband's fortieth birthday. She had called his boss and gotten him Friday off, she'd arranged for someone to watch the kids, and she'd booked the hotel. The week before the trip, she and her husband went over the family finances and discovered they were in a big hole. With these new financial difficulties, Elizabeth felt that she couldn't afford the cost of the trip, but it was the perfect gift. What was she going to do? After talking to her friend Sue, she decided to turn the weekend into a one-night stay at a nearby hotel that was having a special on their rates. Even this trip would cost the exact amount of that week's bonus. It wasn't perfect, but she would make do. That Thursday, she

told her husband she was taking him on an adventure the next day.

When they arrived at the hotel to check in, she was surprised to find a note saying that they had been upgraded to a suite with a fireplace and a hot tub. After they had settled in, a cart with champagne and strawberries was delivered to their suite. The next day, each had a massage, which had already been paid for. Elizabeth and her husband later found out that Sue had decided to surprise them both. When they called to thank her, Sue said that she'd had a fabulous year in her business and wanted to spread it around.

Surprising someone is a particularly delightful kind of giving, one that shows the true happiness of giving. Being new to the practice of surprises myself, I've really noticed how much fun they are for the giver. I still get a smile on my face when I remember leaving a vase of flowers at a neighbor's doorstep or the time I hid $100 in my stepdaughter's backpack as she set off for a summer in Europe. This kind of giving is easy to practice. All it takes is some ingenuity.

The Practices of Radical Generosity

Who can you surprise today with some unexpected generosity act? What are you called to do and for whom?

Do What's Needed

Too many people are ready to carry the stool when the piano needs moving.

—ANONYMOUS

I love this quote so much that I included it here, even though I also used it in *More Random Acts of Kindness*™. It reminds me that even though we may want to pick and choose what to give, going with what's convenient or what's fun, sometimes we just need to do what's needed. Sometimes we just have to get in there and heft that piano, because our friend is moving and needs our help. Perhaps the postage meter broke but the letters need to go out anyway. So we lick three hundred stamps, even though we would rather be answering our email.

I have noticed that there are folks who pitch in and joyfully do what is needed (the givers), people who

Radical Generosity

begrudgingly do it (the resenters), and those who seem always to disappear whenever something extra needs to be done (the withholders). "Not in my job description," they say, which is true.

These resenters and withholders miss out on the joy of pitching in together with others to work on something. They miss the sense of satisfaction when the task is completed. They also miss the happiness that comes from actually doing something you know is needed right now and that will be helpful, even if only in a small way. So much of what most of us do day to day is invisible, and I always relish the times when someone comes along and says, "I need help on this." It makes my efforts more concrete and gives me something specific that I can point to as I think, "I helped make this happen."

The next time someone at the office or home is looking for help, offer to pitch in. Then pay close attention to how it makes you feel.

Look at Your Generosity Teachers

Make yourself necessary to someone.

—RALPH WALDO EMERSON

While writing *Attitudes of Gratitude*, I learned something about myself that I never realized before. I constantly seek out people who have characteristics I want to cultivate. I meet someone and notice her strengths, and if I want to learn this strength, I create a lasting connection with this person. In high school, I latched onto a young teacher because she seemed to have the love of books and the cultured appreciation of the world I desired, and we've been friends ever since. Over the years, I've picked friends who were incredibly loving, so I could learn about love; friends who were exceptionally happy and grateful, so I could learn about happiness and gratitude; and friends who were great mothers, so I could learn about mothering.

The first generosity teacher I had was my father. A big guy of six-foot-two, he inevitably gave me the biggest steak or the extra pork chop instead of keeping it for himself, because I was a meat lover. I noticed him doing it week in and week out, without ever saying

anything about it. I realized that this is how you give without drawing attention to yourself.

My next teacher in giving was Will Glennon. I was twenty-five when we met; he was thirty. He was at the helm of the weekly newspaper that we were both working on. Anyone who has ever worked on a newspaper knows how fast-paced it is—every week, a handful of people must make a sixty-page paper come out on time. I soon noticed how generous Will was whenever someone interrupted him with a question, which was every two minutes or so. He never said, "Go away. I'm busy writing three stories." Instead, he always stopped, smiled, and said, "What can I do for you?" I vowed then and there to cultivate that same kind of graceful generosity when it came to offering help.

Will became my teacher by being generous with money while we were living together. We were well off during some of those years, and he never said no when asked to donate to a cause. He had the money, and he gave it away unthinkingly. Watching him, I realized that this, too, was something to be learned.

I've learned many things about having a giving heart from the people in my life. As Gary Zukav said, "As you come to seek and see the virtues and strengths

The Practices of Radical Generosity

111

and nobilities of others, you begin to seek and see them in yourself also." I've experienced generosity as an abundance of love from Dawna; as the willingness to stick with something difficult with someone no matter how long it takes from Daphne; as the capacity to be truly more concerned with others than yourself from Jackie. As a result of their examples, I have given more in various dimensions than I probably would have previously. I've opened my home to friends in need; I've given trips to friends who could not afford them; I've tried to give my all to the people I work with.

Take a few moments to think about the people who have taught you about living from a giving heart. What specific lessons about radical generosity did you learn? How do you enact them now? What do you still want to learn? Is there someone in your life whom you could learn from? Don't be afraid to ask this person for help. Having your positive qualities acknowledged is a great gift within itself.

Radical Generosity

Include Yourself

We should ask the question whether we are capable of loving ourselves as well as others. Are we treating our body kindly—by the way we eat, by the way we drink, by the way we work? Are we treating ourselves with enough joy and tenderness and peace?

—THICH NHAT HANH

My friend Ginger and I both love to read. We read novels voraciously and then furiously trade them back and forth across three states. Recently she went to the bookstore, she said, and bought me five novels. On the way to mail them, she realized that she was giving me what she really wanted for herself. She had run out of books to read, but somehow it was easier for her to buy them for me than for herself. In the end, she decided that she had bought the books for herself and that she would send them to me when she was finished.

Somehow we think that generosity and self-sacrifice go hand in hand. It's probably a result of ledger-sheet thinking again—if I give something to you, then I must lose something for myself. That

model—that resources are finite and that if I do something nice for you, I must go without—is very deeply entrenched in our thinking. Practicing self-generosity as we deepen our giving helps get us out of the either/or view most of us are stuck in.

Self-generosity is simply doing unto yourself what you would do for others. Many of us give what we most want to receive, and once we recognize that truth, we can easily figure out what we need to give ourselves. Do you spend hours on the phone listening to other people's problems? Perhaps you need to spend some time listening to yourself. Do you love to give flowers to your sweetheart? Perhaps you need to give a bouquet to yourself, for no reason except that it will bring you pleasure.

Self-generosity doesn't have to be confined to the things we do for others; that's just a good place to begin. On a wider scale, self-generosity is the attitude that says, "I am as deserving of my own care and attention as anyone else, and I am going to act toward myself with loving kindness on a regular basis." The forms it takes will be as unique as each of us.

Radical Generosity

The next time you find yourself doing something gener-ous for someone else, also do something nice for your-self. It could be the same thing—you listened to your best friend complain about her marriage for forty-five minutes, so now you will listen to yourself with equal exquisite attention by writing in your journal for forty-five minutes. It could be something different—you wrote a college letter of recommendation for a friend's daughter, so you take yourself out to a beautiful lunch. Give your-self something wonderful the next time you do something wonderful for someone else. Notice the effect it has on you. Is it more likely that you will be generous to yourself and others in the future?

Just Say Yes

Compassion is not quantitative. Certainly it is true that behind every human being who cries out for help there may be a million or more equally entitled to attention. . . . How to determine which of one million sounds surround-ing you is more deserving than the rest? Do not concern yourself in such speculations. You will never know; you

The Practices of Radical Generosity

will never need to know. Reach out and take hold of the
one who happens to be nearest.

—NORMAN COUSINS

I have a very hard time figuring out how to relate to homeless people. Because I'm mad that homelessness exists, I give to organizations that attempt to solve the problem at the fundamental level. I know whatever I put into homeless people's hands or cups will not solve the problem of their homelessness, but there they are—lying on the pavement, sitting on curbs, or standing at freeway on ramps holding signs. I have tried all kinds of things: not giving to anyone no matter what, which seems so cold; giving to everyone no matter what, which isn't possible when you live near a city like San Francisco that has so many homeless people; giving them vouchers for food instead of cash, so the money goes to feeding their bellies and not their addiction; or buying food and giving that. No matter what I do, it doesn't feel right.

My actions don't feel right because homelessness shouldn't exist in such an affluent society. Homelessness makes me uncomfortable, as it should, but my discomfort doesn't absolve me from not taking action. This

sets up an awkward situation, but I found my personal solution. After remembering that someone wise said we should respond "Yes" when asked to help, I decided to follow that advice. If someone on the street asks me for money, I give it. If not, I don't. This strategy may leave out many worthy but silent folk, but, as Norman Cousins stated, just reach out and take hold of one.

Now I always say "Yes" whenever I'm asked to help out. I said "Yes" when someone asked me to host twin fourteen-year-old Vietnamese-French exchange students for a month, and I said "Yes" when I was asked to donate my time to a new spiritual magazine. Instead of volunteering, I wait until asked and then say "Yes." There is more need than any of us can respond to, and this is just my way of deciding where to put my time and attention. I believe that if I am specifically asked, then it is my task to do. This way, I ensure that I respond to the needs all around me, but I don't know what I would do if I were asked to volunteer all the time.

We all need to discover a way to say "Yes." A friend of mine says he figures out what to do by following his generous impulses without second-guessing himself. "If I think about it, I do it, no questions asked," he

The Practices of Radical Generosity

remarked. In his book *Bring the Full Tithe*, Reverend William D. Watley suggests what he calls "Spirit-led giving." "Spirit-led giving occurs when we earnestly seek God's direction as to what we should give and then ask God's help in making a way for us to give it."

> What is your way of deciding when to give and when not? If you're not sure, try my strategy for a while. The next few times you are specifically asked to do something for someone, say "Yes." Then notice whether this criterion for giving suits you or not.

Learn Your No Signals

Almost anything is easier to get into than out of.

—AGNES ALLEN

For years I constantly found myself in the same trap. I wanted to see myself as a loving, giving person. My spouse or kids would ask something of me that I believed a kind, generous person would acquiesce to, so I would say "Yes," truly believing that was how

I felt. Halfway through the experience, I would find myself flying into a rage of resentment, and then I'd feel guilty for being angry. I began to study the pattern and realized that whenever this happened, I really had wanted to say "No" but didn't realize that until my anger signaled my true answer. The trick was to begin to learn my no before I got mad.

Proclaiming that we should say "No" when we feel like it in order to feel the flow of generosity more strongly in our lives is very different from recognizing when we want to say "No." So many of us have been so well trained in compliance that we don't even know until later that our true desire was a big no.

The answer to our true generosity lies in our bodies. Here's a great practice adapted from Andy Bryner and Dawna Markova's *An Unused Intelligence*.

Start by taking five minutes to notice what you are aware of in the present moment. Note the data that your senses experience and speak or write that down. For example, "I feel my feet resting on the floor; I feel my chest rising and falling with my breath; I see a beam of light on the floor; I hear the sound of laughter." Just take down the facts—unembellished sensory data, no comparisons, no analysis, and no stories. Do not, for example, embellish the sound with something like "I hear the sarcastic laughter of some nasty creep."

Now think of an activity you don't like, perhaps something you do begrudgingly or with resentment. Do that activity for a little while, again noticing the sensory data. How does it make you feel? What sensations might be your body's signals of No? Do you get a tightness in the stomach? A pain in the head? A sense of constriction around your heart? A feeling of curling up in general? "When I do this activity, I notice a sinking feeling in the pit of my stomach, as well as a tube of pressure that runs from my stomach to my throat."

Radical Generosity

> Write down what you learned about your body's signals of No. The next time you are doing something you know you don't want to do, notice your body's sensations again. Are they the same or different? Resist telling yourself any story about it or saying, "I shouldn't feel like this." Simply notice what you feel and start keeping a written log of all the ways your body signals you "No."

Keep the Gift in Motion

Follow through on all your generous impulses.

—EPICTETUS

Have you ever thought about where the derogatory term "Indian giver" came from? According to Lewis Hyde's book *The Gift*, it was coined in the mid-1700s when the Puritans were first encountering the Indians in Massachusetts.

"Imagine a scene," writes Hyde. "An Englishman comes into an Indian lodge and his hosts, wishing to make their guest feel welcome, ask him to share a pipe of tobacco. Carved from a soft red stone, the pipe itself

is a peace offering that has traditionally circulated among the local tribes, staying in each lodge for a time but always given away sooner or later. And so the Indians, as is only polite among their people, give the pipe to their guest when he leaves. The Englishman is tickled pink. What a nice thing to send back to the British Museum! A time passes and the leaders of a neighboring tribe come to visit the colonist's home. To his surprise he finds his guests have some expectation in regard to his pipe"—they want him to give it to them! "In consternation the Englishman invents a phrase to describe these people with such a limited sense of private property."

Hyde goes onto say that the person with the limited sense was actually the white man, for the Indians "understood the cardinal property of a gift: whatever we have been given is supposed to be given away again, not kept. . . . As it is passed along, the gift may be given back to the original donor, but this is not essential. In fact, it is better if the gift is not returned but is given instead to some new, third party. The only essential is this: the gift must always move." A gift, says Hyde, is about establishing relationships, and the more it

Radical Generosity

moves, the more connections are made. If a gift stops being given away, it is no longer a gift. (This is such a belief among pre-capitalist cultures that in folktales around the world, a person who tries to keep a gift tends to die.)

Because we live in a capitalist culture where the accumulation of objects is seen to confer status and power, we've lost sight of this notion of gift. Everything we have or "own," however, is a gift from God, the Universe, or the "Great Spirit." Regardless of which source we believe is the giver, the fact that we are alive with the resources we have is an amazing gift. By recognizing this truth, we can begin to see our giving as the Indians did, as a keeping in motion the gift we've received from the benevolence of life.

I am a great believer in learning about yourself by trying various behaviors and noticing the effects they have on you. It's crucially important that when you do any of these practices, including this one, you don't use what you discover to harass and judge yourself. See this as an occasion to learn something that can help you let gifts flow more freely in your life.

The Practices of Radical Generosity

Designate a day as "giving away" day. Pack up all the clothes you no longer wear. Clean your cupboards of all the pots, pans, utensils, and dishes that you don't use. Do the same for the closets where you store the debris from your life—the kids' old toys or the lamp you swore you needed but could never find a place for. Pack it all in bags and take it to your favorite charity. (I like to donate things to the battered women's shelter in my town rather than to a thrift store because the women receive the things for free.)

As you go through the process, notice your train of thought. What objects are you willing to let go of? Which ones must you keep? What thoughts go through your mind as you sort? Do you hold onto something, believing that you will need them later even though you haven't used it yet in ten years? Do you think it's too good to give away even though you don't really want it? Do your possessions make you feel safe?

Practice *Agape*

An overflowing love which seeks nothing in return, agape is the love of God operating in the human heart. At this level, we love men not because we like them, nor because their ways appeal to us, nor even because they possess some type of divine spark; we love every man because God loves him. At this level, we love the person who does an evil deed, although we hate the deed that he does.

—MARTIN LUTHER KING, JR.

Think of someone you don't particularly like but whom you see every day. Don't choose someone who has done something truly awful to you; just choose someone who annoys you by doing something that drives you crazy. You can't stand her and just wish she would drop off the face of your Earth.

You have every right to not like this person. As Martin Luther King, Jr., points out in *From Strength to Love*, Jesus didn't direct us to "like" our enemies, because liking everyone is too hard. Jesus told us to "love" our enemies instead and feel a flow of *agape*, which Dr. King defines as the "understanding and creative, redemptive goodwill for all men," toward every

human being we come across. That's true generosity of spirit.

For whatever reason, this person is in your world right now. You can make it as pleasant an experience for yourself and for her or not. Why not spread as much happiness as you can?

In addition, the fact that she is upsetting you is a clue that you need to learn something through her behavior. Perhaps you envy her certitude and wish you had some of your own, or you need to stand up for yourself more, or you realize that you're longing to say how you feel. Whatever the lesson is, you can't discover it if your heart is closed to her. As long as you think her actions are wrong or bad, you'll stay miserable, because you will never experience the joy of learning what you can from her.

For one day, focus on something you can appreciate about someone you don't like. You don't have to suddenly love them or want to spend time with them. Just notice some trait they have that you can admire, respect, or enjoy. Everyone has something to appreciate. Are they good with handling annoying customers? Do they always remember to bring in bagels for the team? Do they constantly suggest great creative ideas? Look for this trait. Do you feel your heart opening toward them just a crack?

Allow Yourself to Be Appreciated

Giving and receiving should be practiced alternately.

—GESHE CHEHAWA

I know a man who works really hard at being generous and helpful. If you have a need, he goes out of his way to try to fill it. He is greatly appreciated by the people in his life but, ironically enough, he feels completely isolated and unappreciated. At times, he can even fall into martyrdom—feeling he gives so much but gets nothing in return.

The Practices of Radical Generosity

I think I know why he's stuck in this trap—it is very hard for him to receive any kind of appreciation. He's a master at deflection. When someone says, "Thank you," he responds, "It was nothing." If someone gives him a compliment, like "You're really great at fixing the computers," he acts as if nothing has been said. He literally can't take compliments or thanks in any form, so he is starving for it now. He thinks he isn't being appreciated, but he just can't receive what's right in front of him.

While the rest of us may not be suffering as much as he is, most of us are uncomfortable with appreciation. How many of us respond, "It was no big deal," when someone thanks us for something we did? Or say, "This old thing?" when we are complimented on how great we look in the red shirt we're wearing that day. We think it's polite to minimize our efforts or gifts so that the other person won't feel envious or obliged to us. The person on the other side of the exchange, however, feels differently, because he or she is trying to offer something you refuse to receive.

Such "politeness" has insidious effects. Giving and receiving are like an electrical current—two sides of a miraculous exchange of energy—and both need to

occur for the circuit to be complete. Otherwise, as in my friend's case, the connection is never made, and we remain isolated regardless of which end we're on. Either way, it feels lonely.

If you feel as if you are always giving without getting anything in return, try this practice.

> Buy a blank book and, for a month, write down every compliment or thanks someone offers you for something that you've done. At the end of the month, go back and read all the appreciation you've received. When my friend tried this, he was amazed to discover how much he tended to ignore the appreciation he was being offered.

Offer from Overflow

Thousands of candles can be lighted from a single candle, and the life of the candle will not be shortened. Happiness never decreases by being shared.

—BUDDHA

Louise is the founder of a startup. She loves the excitement, the creativity, and the "make it up as you go

along" feeling. She routinely works twelve-hour days, has a husband and two small kids at home, and still manages to give help and support to other women entrepreneurs. She does this all with a joyful spirit. I asked her how she could feel so happy and giving with such a workload. She responded, "My job doesn't leave me much time, but ironically I've discovered that if I take twenty minutes in the morning when I first wake up to be completely quiet and alone, I am then more available to my husband, kids, friends, and coworkers."

How can we give unwaveringly, like a candle, without becoming exhausted, depleted, resentful, or withholding? We can give to ourselves what we give to others; we can actively be on the receiving end; we can realize we can't do everything; and we can say "No" when we mean it. Perhaps the best thing we can do is to give from "overflow," the love we feel flowing from our hearts. To sustain that kind of giving, we need to continually fill ourselves up so that we are full enough to give.

There are two ways to replenish the love we feel flowing from our hearts. First, we need plenty of opportunities in our lives to replenish ourselves. What

gives you joy or nourishes you? I find sitting in a hot tub listening to the birds chatter overhead or walking with a friend around the reservoir by my house and looking at the hills change with the seasons replenishes me. How about you? What's on your list?

Once you have your list, think about how often you do these things. Aside from sitting in the hot tub, I haven't done any of them in months, which explains why I've been feeling exhausted and am not inclined to reach out to anyone else. Make a commitment to yourself to add one thing from your list into your daily routine. A second strategy is developing a practice of renewing ourselves through some of the spiritual energy that is always available. Meditation or prayer is a way many of us get the spiritual renewal we need so we can give from overflow.

Here's a visualization that I like to use, adapted from Sue Patton Thoele's *The Woman's Book of Courage*.

Sit quietly and close your eyes. For a few moments, just notice your breathing. When you feel ready, imagine yourself as a vase. Now imagine white light pouring into your vase, filling you up completely. Imagine the energy from the light soaking into every pore, filling every space, and really take in the experience of fullness. When you are ready, open your eyes and notice how you feel. Today, as you go about your work, notice if having been filled has any effect on your ability to be generous.

Let It Be Easy

Anyone who has got any pleasure at all should try to put something back. Life is like a superlative meal and the world is like the maître d'hôtel. What I am doing is the equivalent of leaving a reasonable tip.

—BRITISH ANIMAL CONSERVATIONIST
GERALD DURRELL

I love this quote. If I think of giving as tipping, it seems so effortless that I'm much more inclined to do

it. When I was younger, I had trouble believing that it was okay if something was easy. From early childhood, I thought the proper approach to life was to take it very seriously and work extremely hard. I had contempt for those who didn't try hard—at school, at church—and was convinced that only good deeds that were extraordinarily difficult were worth anything.

Fortunately, I grew out of that attitude, mostly during my twenties, when a friend said to me, "Just because it's easy doesn't mean you shouldn't do it." Like a Zen *koan*, that remark knocked some sense into me, and, ever since, I've been practicing doing what pleases me and letting it be easy.

That's why I got quite excited when someone emailed me the address of a website called the Hunger Site (*thehungersite.greatergood.com*), which is helping to eliminate hunger around the world. All you have to do is log on and push a button; you don't have to spend a dime or even get up from your desk. This is how the site works—advertisers sponsor at least a week at a time, agreeing to donate the money to purchase half a cup of a staple food in the United Nations World Food Program for each person who logs on and pushes

The Practices of Radical Generosity

a button. More visitors means more donations, which means more advertisers, and a greater quantity of food. The site was started by an individual who wanted to do something about hunger, serving as more proof that an individual can make a huge difference.

What could you do that would be easy for you? Here's an easy way to think about it. As you go about your day, at three separate points ask yourself: What would be easy for me to give? Let yourself think over what the answer is, but, remember, it doesn't have to be hard.

Bestow the Gift of Full Attention

We must not only give what we have; we must give what we are.

—DESIRE-JOSEPH MERCIER

Ted is a friend who recently spent a month in a religious community with about fifty people who live, meditate, and do household work together. "I don't know exactly why," he said to me, "but one of the most amazing things about the experience was how exquisitely people would pay attention when you spoke to them. I would come into the kitchen, say, and strike up a conversation with a person sitting there. Soon I would be pouring out my heart about my pain over the breakup of my marriage and feel so received. And it went both ways—I quickly learned about their struggles and joys as well. I had never experienced anything so intimate in my life."

Ted was experiencing the gift of true presence. Perhaps because the people there spent a great deal of time in silence and in meditation, they were able to bring their full selves and their complete attention to their interactions with one another. What an incredible gift! How often are any of us really, completely present for someone else? Or for ourselves? I often find myself listening to someone with one part of my mind and thinking about how I will respond or, as I get older, trying to remember everything I want to say in response. I listen to someone at the office while I sort papers on my desk, I listen to my husband while I get dressed, or I play with Ana while I try to pick up her room at the same time. I seldom drop

The Practices of Radical Generosity

what I am doing and give my full attention to another human being.

When it comes to paying attention to myself, I can't remember the last time I was completely present for what's really going on inside me. It tends to leak out in dribbles and drabs as I race through my day, and I catch myself stopping at odd moments to think, "I think I'm upset, what am I upset about?" I don't even know if I am happy or sad or even delighted or confused.

The generosity of presence is every bit as valuable as money or advice, because the desire to be truly received is at the heart of every human being. Years ago, studies into the value of psychotherapy found that it wasn't any more effective than talking to a caring friend. Merely being listened to was healing.

Radical Generosity

Sometime soon, really be there for a person who is interacting with you. Stop whatever else you are doing. Sit down with them, or go for a walk. Forget the clock. Really listen, deeply and generously. Resist the impulse to share a story about yourself or to tell the other person what to do. You are there to receive what is being said. When you find your mind wandering, bring it back gently to what he or she is saying. You can even practice on yourself. Ask yourself this very simple question: What is going on for me right now? Write down or tape the answers. Treat yourself as you would the other, just receiving what is being revealed without stories or judgments.

The Practices of Radical Generosity

137

Give Others the Benefit of the Doubt

We can train ourselves to become more yielding, balanced, and flexible, giving up our rigid stances and fixed ideas.

—LAMA SURYA DAS

My husband, Don, and I were in one of those arguments that long-time couples tend to have. The ones where whatever you're angry about is fueled by the fact that you've been in exactly this place saying exactly the same things hundreds of times before. I knew that I was right, and I would bet anything that Don was sure he was. I was making one of my impassioned but logical speeches as I tried to get him to come over to my side, but it was going absolutely nowhere. Suddenly he looked at me and said, "You know, I never thought of it that way before. I think you may have a point." That moment changed everything. I felt like he had really heard me, and I could then see his point of view. Soon we were cuddling on the couch, both feeling closer to one another and to finding a solution than we'd been in months.

It's easy to get stuck in our own perspectives or to be sure we've been wronged or offended by another person on purpose. We think that other person is terrible, mean, or stupid. We're mad, we have every right to be mad, and we're going to stay mad. When we practice generosity, we need to look at giving up our certainty that we are right.

We usually think of generosity in terms of material objects or time—instead of holding on to all of my money, I'm going to give some of it to someone else; instead of holding on to all of my time, I will donate some of it to help others. Generosity is also about letting go of our "damn certitude," as one of my friends calls it, and being willing to entertain the possibility that the other person's perspective has validity, too. When we live from our giving hearts, we stop clinging to our convictions and open ourselves up to the other person's truth. That can change everything.

Just like our money or our time, our notions about ourselves, things, and other people are important to us. They help us navigate through life, make decisions, and move forward. When we bump up against another person, especially when there's conflict, our beliefs can

The Practices of Radical Generosity

really keep us from connecting with one another. We fall into patterns of "You always," "You never," or "I'm always the one who ends up saying I'm sorry, so I'm not going to do it this time." We hold our fixed ideas up like shields, but, instead of protecting us, they just keep us apart.

Next time you find yourself in a conflict with someone, instead of rushing to the barricades, sure that you know the truth of the situation, think to yourself, "Maybe he has a point." By being willing to let go even that much, you can create an opening that will allow better understanding between you.

Share What You Have

Man should not consider his material possessions his own, but common to all, so as to share them without hesitation when others are in need.

—SAINT THOMAS AQUINAS

I have a friend who, along with her sisters, inherited a summer cottage on a lake in Maine when her

parents died. "It has been," she told me ruefully, "quite an exercise in sharing. At first, it was used on a first-come, first-served basis. But then one of my sisters complained that she hardly ever used it, while my other sister and I used it all the time, so she wanted first crack at the peak holiday times. Then there were the cleaning and repair issues: someone would break something and not replace it, and later there would be a tracking-down of the wrongdoer by a resentful sister forced to rectify the situation. I've been surprised at how difficult it's been and what feelings it stirs up."

As my friend discovered, sharing provides many opportunities to learn about ourselves and our capacity for generosity, possessiveness, self-righteousness, and cooperation. By sharing, we offer our resources to one another and are aided in return; we also treat the world more gently by avoiding the mindless accumulation of too many material things. Despite the insistence of well-crafted commercials, we do not need all the latest toys. One lawn mower can service many lawns; one cottage can shelter many families.

Most of us tend not to share as much as we can. My mother claims that whenever she borrows something she breaks it, so she doesn't want the burden of

that on her head. I've tried sharing a camcorder with friends and have found this quite inconvenient. I can't just use it any time I want, because I have to schedule it with them. I have happily shared my washer and dryer with my tenants for years, but I suppose that if they weren't naturally considerate, I would have to negotiate with them about when it was okay for them to traipse across my house with their clothes and run the very loud machines.

Sharing requires us to be in relationship with one another. We must negotiate the cottage schedule or call and ask if we can borrow the VCR. If the sharing is unequal, we have to tread through all of our—and their—uncomfortable feelings.

In our world, sharing is important for two reasons. The Earth simply can't support everyone having everything they want. We must learn to share, or we will destroy all life. It is also important that we allow ourselves opportunities to experience the feelings, good and bad, that sharing creates. It forces us to reach out and become less separate. When we choose to share something, we stretch our souls and spare the Earth—at least a little.

Become aware of your willingness or unwillingness to share by taking a few moments to go around your house and look at your things. Imagine that each of these things has a rubber band around it that is attached to you. For each item, notice how tight or loose the rubber band is. Which things are more closely attached to you? Which are looser? When I do this, I discover that the two things tightly attached to me are my hot tub and my photos. The rest of my "stuff" is much more loosely attached.

What's the Radically Generous Thing to Do?

It's not the earthquake
That controls the advent of a different life
But storms of generosity . . .

—BORIS PASTERNAK

I've been practicing generosity for almost twenty years—not perfectly, by any means, but certainly as something I strive for as I go about my days and weeks. The formula I follow is one I described elsewhere in

The Practices of Radical Generosity

this book—if someone asks me for something, I say "yes" if I at all can.

During the same time frame, I met Vicki Saunders. She was an attendee at a retreat that my colleagues and I used to run every two months at Robert Redford's Sundance resort. Vicki and I stayed in touch on and off over years as she lived a life of an entrepreneur and I a coach for entrepreneurs and executives. I experienced the generosity of her referring me client after client, an unbelievably invaluable gift to me as I am terrible at marketing myself.

At some point along the way, she started talking to me about the concept of SheEO, a new model for funding and supporting women entrepreneurs. I've had the privilege to think with her about the idea and not only see it birthed in Canada and begin to spread around the world but also be part of the team that's guiding, supporting, and mentoring the funded ventures. And what amazing companies they are—developing beeswax wrap that allows food to breathe (Abeego); creating a model for supporting family fishermen (Skipper Otto's); hiring at-risk youth to make and deliver lunches to gain practical, on the job expe-

rience (The Town Kitchen); inventing a third-party college sexual assault recording and reporting system to better empower survivors (Project Callisto)—and that's just to name four of them. SheEO is a bold and visionary idea.

Vicki has always maintained that the concept of Radical Generosity was at the heart of SheEO. And we've had lots of conversations about what that might mean. Recently she told me of a practice she's started to do (see next page). Hum, I thought, I should be doing it, too.

Wow. What a life-changing practice. It's something about adding the word "radical," of course. Yesterday I gave one hundred dollars to a stranger in response to my asking myself that question. Mostly, however, it helps me stay gracious in lines and with cashiers when I am in a rush and to be kinder to my sweetie. Ironically, it's also helped me to say "no" more easily—because often the person I need most to be radically generous to is myself!

The Practices of Radical Generosity

As you go about your day, in every situation you find yourself whether it's a request by someone, a traffic jam, or an irritation with your loved one, ask yourself, "What's the radically generous thing to do now?" Then do whatever it is your mind comes up with. Notice how it makes you feel.

Pass It On to Your Kids

A seed will only become a flower if it gets sun and water.

—PSYCHIATRY PROFESSOR LOUIS GOTTSCHALK

I recently heard a story about how the Onondaga people used to teach their children about generosity. When it was time for someone to learn, the tribe would gather in a circle. The child would be brought into the center of the circle and given wonderful things to drink. After he had his fill, a voice would come from outside the circle, saying, "I'm thirsty, I'm thirsty," and the child would be encouraged to take the drink to the thirsty person. The child would be brought back into the circle and fed fabulous food. After, he would hear a voice

outside the circle, saying, "I'm hungry, I'm hungry." Again, the child would leave the circle to feed the hungry person. The child would return to the circle and be given beautiful, warm clothes to wear. Again he would hear a voice, crying, "I'm cold, I'm cold," and he would gather up clothes and help dress the freezing person.

Ever since contemporary social scientists have concluded that giving behavior is innate, they've become very interested in the study of altruism, asking why some people help while others don't, and which circumstances lead to help being offered. They have begun to study the childhoods of individuals who have demonstrated a high degree of altruism. The social scientists found that these folks had loving parents who instilled in them a healthy sense of self-esteem and self-efficacy. Their parents also instilled a strong sense of right and wrong; like the Onondaga Indians, altruists were taught specifically to be generous.

Most important, these folks had parents who modeled generosity. Studies of volunteers have also found that the majority of dedicated volunteers had parents who were also volunteers. Like any other aspect of parenting, we not only have to say what's right, we have to do what's right in order for our kids to learn. Instead of

The Practices of Radical Generosity

just telling them to be generous, we must demonstrate clearly and consistently our own generosity.

At Christmastime, I always took my stepkids and my child to a toy store, where I let them pick out a hundred dollars' worth of toys to give away to Toys for Tots. They really got a kick out of thinking about the pleasure other kids would get from their selections. When I was a kid, we used to make up food baskets for families in need at Thanksgiving and go Christmas caroling at senior centers.

While these actions are wonderful, they only happen once a year, which isn't enough to instill the giving habit. My friend Dawna's grandmother used to do this simple practice with her.

When you are doing something enjoyable with your child, like swimming, say something like, "We're having such fun. Let's take a minute to send this feeling of fun to all those kids who have never been in a pool." This way, they'll learn, just as the Native American kids did, that giving comes from a sense of well-being and that giving enhances the abundance that the giver is experiencing, rather than diminishing it.

Cultivate Spiritual Generosity

Regularly ask yourself, "How are my thoughts, words, and deeds affecting my friends, my spouse, my neighbor, my child, my employer, my subordinates, my fellow citizens? Am I doing my part to contribute to the spiritual progress of all I come into contact with?" Make it your business to draw out the best in others by being an exemplar yourself.

—EPICTETUS

Earlier in this section, I mentioned Jackie Waldman, the author of *The Courage to Give*. Jackie is one of the most remarkable people I have ever met in my life. Every time I speak with her, I hang up the phone committed to becoming more loving and generous. It's not that she lectures me on giving—far from it. Instead, she is such an example of the beauty and joy of selflessness that I am inspired to become the same.

All authors want their books to do well. Some want money, others want fame. Still others want to get their message across. While Jackie wants her message about the gifts of volunteerism to spread, she really wants her books to do well because of the people profiled

in them. She has generously given away a major portion of her royalties to the charities associated with the people profiled, and if her book does well, they will prosper.

There are many different ways to be generous—monetarily, physically, emotionally, and, yes, spiritually. Although we generally don't think about spiritual generosity, it is as real and important as any of the other forms. It is, as Epictetus points out, the offering of the essence of yourself to other people as a spiritual model, not because you've set yourself up on a pedestal to be adored but because you've striven to live according to your values as much as possible. Gandhi, Mother Teresa, and Nelson Mandela are all examples of this kind of generosity. Through the power of their spiritual purity (which is not to say they didn't have faults or made mistakes), they had a huge impact on the fate of the world. If we think of their footsteps as a way of marking a path for us to walk along in our own way and at our own pace, their impact and their example become inspiring rather than daunting.

We don't have to try to liberate whole countries or heal lepers in order to cultivate our own unique brand

Radical Generosity

of spiritual generosity. We only have to ask ourselves Epictetus's first question, and we touch the transformative power of radical generosity.

For one week, try asking yourself this question before you go to sleep at night: How are my thoughts, words, and deeds affecting my friends, my spouse, my neighbors, my child, my employer, my subordinates, my fellow citizens? Notice what your response is, and let whatever's true for you be okay. Don't use this as occasion to browbeat or guilt-trip yourself, because guilt will just paralyze you. With great compassion for yourself, just notice your answers to the question. Then notice how the answers change over the week. If you're like me, you'll notice that on some days, you've had a more positive effect, and on others, a less positive one. Notice without judgment. The more we accept ourselves exactly as we are, the more room we create for change. At the end of the week, decide if this is a practice you would like to continue.

The Practices of Radical Generosity

Try "Sending and Taking"

Even the thought of giving, the thought of blessing or a simple prayer, has the power to affect others.

—DEEPAK CHOPRA

When my father was dying, I was three thousand miles away and had adopted my one-year-old daughter only three weeks before. I visited a few times, but it was important that I be at home bonding with my little one who had been abandoned and neglected. I would call from afar, feeling terrible that there wasn't more I could do.

Sometimes there is nothing we can do to help someone else. We live too far away, have other pressing obligations, or there is nothing we could do anyway. Often, if it is a problem of overwhelming proportions, we end up feeling hopeless. We see reports, for instance, of mudslides and mass death in Central America. Or in Asia. Or our own backyards. We send money or perhaps collect clothes and blankets, but that is such a small drop in the bucket compared to the suffering being experienced.

Radical Generosity

Most of us in such situations shut down and close off our hearts so that we don't have to feel the pain of others. We ignore it and put it out of our minds. When we shut down to others'—or our own—pain, we also shut down to the possibility of joy. It's all or nothing— either we feel both abundance and loss, both the majesty of life and the truth of death, or we don't fully feel either of them. A teacher of mine once said, "To touch the ten thousand joys, you must be willing to face the ten thousand sorrows."

With practice, we can learn to keep our hearts open to both the beauty and the sorrow and live more awake and more available to others. One way to practice this openness when you are feeling in despair about the suffering of someone or the state of the world is to offer a prayer. Recent research proves that prayer works, including a study done on 393 heart attack patients; 192 were prayed for without their knowing about it, and the rest were not. All other treatment was exactly the same. Out of the group that was prayed for, there were fewer fatalities and more rapid recoveries, showing that our blessings and best wishes can make a difference.

The Practices of Radical Generosity

A Tibetan Buddhist practice takes this one step further. It's called *tonglen*, or sending and taking. This extremely powerful practice in generosity allows you to breathe in the suffering of the world and then breathe out peace and happiness. You can do it for yourself, for someone you know who is going through a hard time, or for people you've never met who've experienced some tragedy.

As the Buddhist teacher Pema Chödrön says in *The Wisdom of No Escape*, this practice "is the opposite of avoidance. You are completely willing to acknowledge and feel pain—your own pain, the pain of a dear friend, or the pain of a total stranger—and on the out-breath, you let the sense of . . . opening, the sense of spaciousness, go out." You don't try to analyze anything or figure out anything. You just feel the feeling and then send its opposite.

Because we tend to move away from pain and hold on to pleasure, this practice reverses the trend—it can be a bit of a challenge, at least in the beginning. So I strongly suggest that to begin with, you do this for yourself. The next time you are experiencing something difficult—depression, sorrow, fear,

physical pain—-sit quietly and breathe in your suffering. Then send yourself all the happiness and peace you can. Maybe you don't feel happy or peaceful in this moment, but you can connect to the happiness you've felt in the past and send yourself that.

This is the most generous act I know of—to be willing to take in suffering and radiate joy. No amount of money given to charity can equal it, and you can practice it anytime, anywhere. All it takes is the willingness of the giving heart.

To practice *tonglen*, you need to sit quietly and, on the in-breath, allow yourself to open to the pain, discomfort, and suffering they are feeling. On the out-breath, allow yourself to open to feelings of joy, well-being, tenderheartedness, and peacefulness, and then send them into the world to be experienced by those who are suffering. Do this for as long or as short a time as feels right to you.

The Practices of Radical Generosity

An Ever-Expanding Spiral

I don't want to be saved. I want to be spent.

—FRITZ PERLS

A friend once told me a story about his grandmother. She was always a generous person—generous with her laughter, with her fabulous cherry pies, and with her time as a tutor to adults who couldn't read. Every time he went to see her as a young adult, she had given away something else from her apartment—to the TV repairperson, to the mail carrier, to the young girl from apartment 2G who was moving into her own place for the first time. Finally, when he arrived to find the dining room set being hauled out the door, he spoke up. "I said I was upset because I didn't want to see her with nothing left," he confessed to me. "She sat me down and said, 'Sweetheart, the key thing is timing. I would love to time it so that the day I die I have nothing left.'"

This wise grandmother understood a profound truth—we can't take anything with us when we die. In a sense, when we die, all that we have not given away dies with us unshared. All the smiles, all the laughter, all our capacity for empathy and compassion, even all our knowledge and wisdom. Giving everything away ensures that it—and we—truly lives on, in a grand-child who continues to bake our secret recipe for cherry pie, in a homeless person we will never meet who wears our winter coat, or in the woman who can read.

Years ago, another friend's wise grandmother taught her that life is like a spiral on which we must walk. She called it the Wisdom Trail. We keep circling the same issues over and over, but we hope that, with wisdom, we'll be at a different level the next time we encounter them. I thought about that when I first heard about the Buddhist theory of the three levels of generosity.

The first level is tentative giving, where we're not sure we want to give. Perhaps we have an old sofa that we're thinking of giving to Goodwill, but we hesitate:

What if someday we need it? In the end, we decide it's okay to let go of the sofa, and we experience freedom and happiness. That feels pretty good, we think. Maybe we'll do it again.

This realization makes it easier to walk along the spiral to the second level, which is brotherly or sisterly giving, a sharing of both ourselves and our resources as if to a loved one. With this kind of giving, instead of hesitation, we feel a sense of "I have this and you can have some, too." We experience a sense of openness, friendship, and joy.

The third level is royal giving, a highly developed sense of generosity where we take such delight in the welfare and happiness of others that we give the best of what we have, rather than just some of it. This is where we put others first, not because we're self-sacrificing but because it feels great. With this kind of giving, writes Jack Kornfield, "it is as if we become a natural channel for the happiness of all around us." The cherry pie-making grandmother was at this level, and because she was living in touch with the inner state of abundance, she could feel comfortable giving everything away.

An Ever-Expanding Spiral

We can't vault to royal giving with the force of our will. Rather, as we walk the trail of our lives, attuned to the opportunities to give tentatively as well as feeling great compassion for ourselves whenever we feel withholding, we will trace an ever-expanding spiral of giving. Our hearts will open to their fullest, and we will eventually rest, like kings and queens, in the abundance of spirit that is our true nature.

Acknowledgments

First and foremost, my thanks goes to my friend Dawna Markova, who once again generously shared her stories, practices, and thoughts with me. My home is full with your gifts, my head is full with your teachings, and my heart is full with your loving. You epitomize "a giving heart."

I was lucky enough to spend some time with my brilliant and loving friend Ann Baker just as I was beginning this book. Our conversations, and her insights and stories, helped ripen my thinking and my trust that I was covering the bases. The generosity of your friendship over the years is one of my greatest gifts.

My thanks as always goes to my other teachers, both those whom I am privileged to call friends and family, and those whom I've learned from in books and lectures: Vincent Ryan, Daphne Rose Kingma, Molly Fumia, Jackie Waldman, Joel and Michelle Levey, Sue Patton Thoele, Jack Kornfield, Sylvia Boorstein, Thich Nhat Hanh, Sharon Salzburg, and Pema Chödrön, as well as the work of Vicki Saunders and SheEO.

My thinking about the nature of generosity was also enriched by the books *The Gift* by Lewis Hyde, *Generosity* by Tibor R. Machan, *Beyond Fear* by Aeeshah Ababio-Clottey and Kokomon Clottey, *Sacred Practices for Conscious Living* by Nancy J. Napier, *The Wisdom of No Escape* by Pema Chödrön, *The Pleasure Zone* by Stella Resnick, *Leadership and the New Science* by Margaret J. Wheatley, *Writing for Your Life* by Deena Metzger, and *Awakening the Buddha Within* by Lama Surya Das. The audiotape *Generosity of the Heart* by Jack Kornfield also prompted further reflection.

Thanks also to my family, who let me write about them and graciously gave of their time so that I could write.

A deep bow of thanks to all the folks who worked with me at Conari Press when this book was originally published in 2000 as *The Giving Heart*, as well as all

the folks at Red Wheel/Weiser who took over Conari Press and have kept the books I've birthed alive and were willing to bring back this book in a new form. Publishing was never easy, but, more and more, it is an act of radical generosity to the world.

Acknowledgments

About the Author

Known internationally as a change expert, M. J. has worked as an executive coach, thinking partner, and mentor for the past seventeen years, helping executives and entrepreneurs maximize success. She has a wide range of clients around the world, from one-person startups to executives of global corporations such as Royal Dutch Shell, Microsoft, HP, and many others. She currently serves as one of the heads of the program guides for SheEO, an organization offering new funding and support models for women entrepreneurs.

The founder and former CEO of Conari Press, she is one of the creators of the bestselling Random Acts of Kindness series and the author of eight books, including *Habit Changers, Surviving Change You Didn't Ask For, The Happiness Makeover, Attitudes of Gratitude*, and *The Power of Patience.*

She holds a BA cum laude from Cornell University in psychology and is a member of the International Coaching Federation and the International Positive Psychology Association. Articles on her work have appeared in the *New York Times, USA Today,* the *Wall St. Journal, HuffPost, Inc.com, Forbes.com, Good Housekeeping, Town & Country, Yoga Journal,* and many other publications and websites.

To Our Readers

Red Wheel/Weiser, publishes books on topics ranging from spirituality, personal growth, and relationships to women's issues, parenting, and social issues. Our mission is to publish quality books that will make a difference in people's lives—how we feel about ourselves and how we relate to one another. We value integrity, compassion, and receptivity, both in the books we publish and in the way we do business.

Our readers are our most important resource, and we appreciate your input, suggestions, and ideas about what you would like to see published.

Visit our website at *www.redwheelweiser.com* to learn about our upcoming books and free downloads, and be sure to go to *www.redwheelweiser.com/newsletter* to sign up for newsletters and exclusive offers.

You can also contact us at *info@rwwbooks.com.*

Red Wheel/Weiser, LLC
65 Parker Street, Suite 7
Newburyport, MA 01950
www.redwheelweiser.com